A Stockbridge
Homecoming

常存我心

CHINA TO AMERICA

A Stockbridge
Homecoming

PENELOPE S. DUFFY

bright sky press
Albany, Texas

bright sky press
Albany, Texas

Duffy, Penelope S. (Penelope Starratt), 1948-
    A Stockbridge homecoming : China to America / Penelope S. Duffy
        p. cm.

10 9 8 7 6 5 4 3 2 1

    ISBN 978-1-931721-84-4 (sftcvr: alk. paper)
        Duffy, Penelope S. (Penelope Starratt), 1948- 2. Children of
missionaries—China—Biography. 3. Children of missionaries—United States—Biography.
I.Title.

BV3427.D84 A3 2001
915.104'55092273--dc22
[B]

                                                      2006014153

Cover design: Whittington & Co.
Austin, Texas

Book design: Richard Oriolo

Printed in China by Asia Pacific Offset

NOTE TO THE READER

The events recounted in this book are based on recollections of my family and on over 150 letters in my possession that were written at the time the events took place.

Names of some of the people who may still be living and who could not be contacted in the course of writing this book have been changed.

Over the course of the shared history between China and the West, a number of different systems have been developed for transcribing Chinese into the Roman alphabet. The Pinyin system, currently in use, was developed in the latter half of the 20th Century by the People's Republic of China. The spelling of Chinese names and locations in this book, however, are based on the Wade-Giles system of transcription, which was in use at the time the events depicted in this book took place. Thus, for example, using the Wade-Giles system, Beijing (in Pinyin) is transcribed as Peking; the Pinyin name Mao Ze Dong is transcribed as Mao Tse-Tung, as it was in the 1940s.

ACKNOWLEDGMENTS

There are many people who made this book possible. My heartfelt thanks to Betsy Elias for envisioning the possibilities and guiding me through the process and to my agent, Barbara Bowen, whose expertise, good sense, and consistent support made the writing a pleasure. I am most grateful to Kate Hartson and Rue Judd at Bright Sky Press for all their hard work and dedication to the book. I appreciate the editorial comments made by those who read early drafts of the manuscript including Betsy Elias, Anne Healy, Peg Kelly, Sunday Kornye, the Inklings, my sister, Patty Starratt, members of the Duffy clan, and especially, my husband Joe, who is always my "first reader." I wish to thank my sisters, Polly and Patty, for their memories and encouragement, and my friends and family for their unfailing love and support. Finally, I would like to thank parents - my father for his gifts as a writer and recorder of events and for the love that shines through his letters, and my mother who gave me the letters before she died saying, "I know you will know what to do with these."

A Stockbridge Homecoming

One

*I*DON'T REMEMBER anything about the events I am about to tell, this is true. Except the doll. I do remember the doll. I imagine it was snowing when we arrived because it snowed in the years afterward at Christmas time. I imagine we drove up in an old gray Plymouth because that is the first car I remember us having, though the car was probably borrowed. I imagine the car, slow and heavy, making its muffled way down a deserted Main Street before my father eased it into the driveway. I imagine that we sat there a moment staring open-mouthed at the house before climbing out onto the plowed drive. But of the exact events I have no real memory because I was too young. The events themselves, however, are true. They have been told and retold within the family, and in so doing, have shaped us all. I do not remember these events, but some fifty years later, the memory of them is as bright as the yellow light cast from the windows of the house onto the snowy lawn on that December 22, in the year of 1949, in the town of Stockbridge, Massachusetts.

Our presence in Stockbridge on that particular night was no less miraculous than the fact of our return to the United States or my father finding work in my parents' beloved New England. But most miraculous of all was the fact that our family was again together after nearly a year's separation in China – a year in which days had lengthened into weeks, and weeks had marched into months of mounting uncertainty, until in the end, we were not sure we would ever see my father again.

Our journey began in the fall of 1948 as the Communist Revolution spread through war-ravaged China. But its seeds had been planted several years earlier in a white frame house in Lincoln, Massachusetts. Late one evening my father walked into the kitchen, and instead of changing out of his clerical collar and black suit into his well-worn sweater, he sat right down at the table. As my mother pulled a steaming pot of Boston baked beans out of the oven, he asked her, "How would you like to go to China?"

China? Timbuktu? Not much difference. She laughed at such foolishness. But looking up as she lifted the cover off the bean pot, she saw his eyebrows raised and that same how-would-you-like-a-puppy smile he'd had a few months before when he'd pulled a wriggling Newfoundland puppy from a basket on the porch. That little handful was now eighty-five pounds of black fur snoring peacefully by the door.

She sat down. She replaced the cover on the squat little bean pot. She stared at it for several moments, then cocked her head and looked at him. She said quietly, "Whatever are you talking about?" And there in the kitchen of the St. Anne's Church rectory, he told her just what he was talking about.

A flurry of excited words poured out about a position at a Christian university in Central China, a university badly in need of trained professors; a position teaching theology and philosophy, a job in which he could put his doctoral studies to good use, a place where he could help spread the kind of liberal Christianity that fed his soul and fired his heart. He told her how it would be a new beginning for him, for them, how they would be even more of a team through the opportunity to help others as part of the Anglican Mission in Central China. "We wouldn't be going over there to save souls or convert people, but to be examples, to live out our faith, to affect the lives of young people through scholarship and service." In short, he said it was the opportunity of a lifetime.

He paused for a breath, the features of his face fixed in eager intensity. Ma stared at him, and when he reached for a napkin to wipe his mouth, she turned to the beans and removed the cover. She lifted the spoon and dipped it in and out of the pot, slowly turning the little oval shapes over in the deep brown sauce. Through the rising steam she envisioned herself with two small children traipsing across oceans and time zones into the misty reaches of the unknown.

Here they were, just a few years into their first parish, in a dear little town in their home state. Here they were, with two little girls, ages three and four, dancing through their days. She thought of what the two of them had been through to get them to this little haven. Thought of the first time she saw him, thirteen years ago – nineteen years old, flat on his back in Medical II, the polio rehab ward of Massachusetts

Memorial Hospital. Like all the others, he'd whistle and call out to the nurses, especially the good-looking ones, signaling a desperate need for a back rub, a temperature taken, a blanket adjusted, anything, anything at all. The young men in the rows and rows of white cots were glad to be alive, glad to be breathing on their own. Some, like my father, had had the last rites said over them as they lay helpless in their iron lungs, but now they were the lucky ones. They'd made it to Medical II. They could breathe on their own. Maybe they'd be able to walk. The nurses understood that the specter of wheelchairs, crutches, and heavy iron braces was kept at bay by the boisterous hoots and hollers and other expressions of pent-up anxiety and pent-up hopes.

She'd move down the ward, all crisp, white-starched business, but something about him softened her, something sad. Like the others, he'd grab her hand while she ministered to him, flirting, saying things he shouldn't. But when she would skirt good-naturedly around such foolishness, when she'd withdraw her hand to re-adjust his lifeless legs or fluff his pillow, she sometimes caught a look in those pale blue eyes that made her want to stay and fill the emptiness. After hours, in the student nurse dormitory, she'd reflect on the way a strand of his blond hair fell into a damp curl against the white pillowcase, the way his features went slack as she'd move on to the next patient, the stillness of his hands, the way he called her an angel of mercy and seemed to mean it. Something, something so earnest, so full of longing, something beyond the bravado and high jinks drew her in, made her flush, made her steps light.

The doctors said he wouldn't walk. She told him he would. He came to believe her. Told her he would walk her down the aisle. One day, in a shaft of light on the sun porch of Medical II, an attendant helped him to his feet out of the wooden wheelchair. Two doctors, dappled in doubt, watched as he stood wavering, his tall, thin frame temporarily locked in place by the brace. Then the coiled concentration took over as he took his first stiff, clanking step toward her square hands. Later, after he was discharged from the hospital in a wheelchair, they practiced – he and she – walking as one, he leaning his hip against hers, up and down the hard sands of Wollaston Beach and Nantasket. Two years later, on June 2, 1937, he walked her down the aisle in a tiny ceremony attended by their mothers, one of her brothers, and her best friend.

Now she sat stirring the beans, thinking of those walks, of the first beans she'd cooked – those hard little nuggets that she'd cried over until he made her laugh. What do they eat in China?

He was talking again, earnest, enthusiastic, pleading, but fair – wanting her to share his vision, unwilling to uproot if she did not. It would be safe, he told her. It was 1946. The Japanese occupation of China had ended with their surrender to MacArthur over a year ago.

She put him off with a thousand practical reasons all through dinner. She started washing the plates with sudsy efficiency, refusing to discuss it further. He came up behind her, wrapped his arms around her, and started singing, "With someone like you, a pal so good and true, I'd like to leave it all behind and go and find, some sweet little nest...." She shook her head in resignation, but with something inside of her tingling and alive at the adventure of it. Several weeks later they were making arrangements for the move.

He informed the bishop, informed the vestry, and started lessons in Chinese. She organized every practical aspect of the move, separating the things they would take, the things they would store, finding a home for Cinder, the Newfoundland. They visited family and friends. And at last they found themselves on a train headed to San Francisco where they had booked passage on a ship to Hong Kong. There is a picture of them in front of a car that they had rented in San Francisco to drive along Route 1. They appear to be at the water's edge. My mother, looking out toward the Pacific, is holding her hat firmly against the wind. In front of the folds of her billowing skirt my sisters, Polly and Patty, dressed in identical plaid skirts, dark woolen sweaters and matching tams, face the camera with serious little faces.

Nearly a month later they stood on the deck of the old troop transport ship that had taken them halfway around the world as the waters broke over its bow in Victoria Harbor, Hong Kong. The treeless hills of Lan Tao faintly echoed the outline of the coastal California mountains that they had left behind on Route 1. Little else would remind them of home. Below them, freighters, Chinese junks, sampans, local steamers, ferries, rafts, and rowboats coursed in and around one another in a miraculous choreography of near collision. Bright flags of blue, white, and black laundry fluttered beside paper lanterns in the shapes of dragons and fish on what seemed like acres of houseboats listing one against another at the wharf.

The harbor streets vibrated with the clatter of rickshaw wheels, piercing police whistles, shouts of harbor officials, cries of barter, pleas of beggars, greetings and farewells. Squawking chickens and ducks were juggled along in bam-

boo carriers, bicycles darted in and out of the crowds, coolies
charged up with high-pitched offers of transport and help
with baggage. Chinese men and women blurred by, some in
traditional trousers and padded blue jackets, some in western
dress, their animated interchange creating little cyclones of
unfamiliar dialect as they passed by. A number of rumpled
and confused Europeans and Americans looked anxiously for
their contacts as they made their way toward the customs
agents. Others managed the disembarkation process with off-
hand aplomb.

Ma was among the pale and unsteady, having heaved her
way through the entire voyage in a constant state of motion
sickness. A sailor helped her down the swaying gangplank of
the launch and led her to a bench. There she held a handkerchief to her forehead with one hand and clutched the girls
tight with the other as my father stood in line at Customs. At
the other end of the complicated process, they were relieved
to see several members of the Anglican Church Mission waving in excited greeting. Welcoming hugs were given and
arrangements made to secure the trunks for transport to the
interior a few days hence. Then they were shepherded
through the noise and confusion to a waiting car ready to
take them to the Church Guest House across the city. As the
car made its slow progress, the crush and press of life rushing up against itself was played out on paved streets against
a backdrop of colorful storefronts, open markets, stately government buildings, and graceful hotel fronts. A glimpse
through their open doors revealed elegant lobbies lined with
potted plants and rows of ceiling fans, slowly cycling air
through British formalities of high tea and diplomacy.

The Church Guest House, their temporary destination,

had been set up by the Church of England as a kind of way station for transient missionaries on their way in or out of China. Situated on Upper Albert Road, it was directly across from the long lawns and stone steps of Victoria Park, a piece of the British Empire that, unknown to my mother then, would one day become as familiar as the ponds and paths of the Boston Public Garden.

As they pulled up, the pale stucco facade of the Guest House took on a creamy glow in the thick, golden light of late afternoon. Inside, a genteel lobby gave way to a broad staircase leading to two stories of sparsely furnished, dormitory-styled rooms. There they were greeted by the short and kindly Dr. Harth who ran the Guest House. He welcomed them with, "Alfred, Anne, it's so good to meet you. How was the trip? Made it all in due time, eh?" Then he bent down to the two little girls, each holding one of Ma's hands.

"Now, which of you is Polly and which one is Patty?" he asked.

Patty, the more talkative one, said, "I am Patty and she is Polly. You can tell because I have blond hair and Polly has red."

"Ah, yes, Polly has auburn hair," he replied. "Welcome to Hong Kong, young ladies." With pronounced formality he shook each of their hands in turn, which pleased them no end.

Shown to a room and settling their belongings, the heave of the ship still with them, they washed up at the nearest bathroom and then attempted a brief rest. Dad, characteristically, fell instantly into a deep sleep. Ma, who always took pride in her "great powers of recovery," was soon up and about, brushing out my sisters' hair and getting them and herself into clean clothes for dinner. An hour or so later at the long tables in the communal dining room, a sense of home seeped through the staggered flashes of their journey as grace was said, as heads were bowed, as thanks was given.

Conversation at dinner centered on the Mission in Wuchang where they were headed, on news from the States, and on small talk. After dinner, Ma took the girls up to bed. Dr. Harth invited Dad and Dr. Cahill, a physician on his way back to England, and several others into his private quarters. In the soft lamplight over a pot of Chinese tea, they talked a bit about the political situation in China.

"Not surprisingly, now that the war is over, the power-struggle between the Chinese Communists and Chiang Kai-shek's Nationalists has picked up where it left off," Dr. Harth began, sucking in deep draughts to get his pipe going. "It seems Mao's forces gained further strongholds in the North during the war," he continued, flicking the metallic lighter shut with a snap.

"As you probably know," Dr. Cahill addressed Dad, "Chiang's Kuomintang army is trying to contain the Communists in Manchuria – with American aid, of course. The problem is the never-ending corruption in the Nationalist regime. Graft, intrigue, inept leadership, all the rest."

"I think General Stillwell saw that well enough during the war. But the Generalissimo and Madame Chiang certainly hold sway with some of the State Department crowd," Dad said.

"I dare say, at this point, as you Americans learned during the war, Chiang is the only game in town – the only hope for an eventual republic. And, of course, he's a known entity and a Christian. The Nationalists control the south and central areas, including Wuchang. . . . " Dr. Harth's voice trailed off. Gray-white curls of smoke meandered up from his pipe.

An earnest young missionary just back from Changsha broke in. "But a lot of Chiang's control is through dubious alliances with local warlords. The real problem is that all this fighting diverts Chiang from needed reform and rebuilding. Things are pretty inefficient. That's nothing new. But eight years of Japanese occupation have devastated China – I read the other day that she lost some three million soldiers and eighteen million civilians."

"Yes," added Dr. Cahill, "and this attempt to rout the Communists and the focus on military aims have left the rebuilding of China a pretty barren concept pitted against the realities of inflation and hunger. But I dare say, it has to be done, and things go on, regardless."

Dr. Harth looked toward Dad and said, "I shouldn't worry about it relative to the Mission. Huachung University will soon be thriving again under the leadership of Dr. Wei. It needs professors like you, of course, but the students are back and excited."

It was the Chinese people, not the political fortunes of China's leaders, that captured the rest of the conversation that night. It little mattered who ruled a single village or all of China as long as the work of the clergy, the physicians, teachers, nurses, nuns, and the rest who served the Missions could continue. They were firm in their belief that their work would indeed continue, so great was the need, so strong their commitment. The talk of Mission work, of the University, of the schools, and bits of gossip about friends in the interior went on long after discussions of the fluctuations of war and politics had been dismissed. Dr. Harth inquired about the topic of my father's doctoral thesis, which Dad intended to write while in Wuchang. Eventually the conversation came to a close, and everyone retired for the night.

It is uncertain exactly how long my parents remained at the Guest House, but it was not more than a week. On the morning of their departure, Dr. Harth found Polly staring at a wall map of China from the doorway to his rooms. He invited her in, and at her request, showed her where Wuchang was on the map. "Here it is, way up here, deep in the interior – about six hundred miles to the north." He held a pointer, and Polly watched as he traced the train route from Canton north to Wuchang. "You'll be living right here, at the confluence of the Yangtze and the Han Rivers. Do you know about the Yangtze?"

"No."

"Well, it is a great and powerful river, Miss Polly. Sometimes it is known as the 'Long River.' It is almost four thousand miles from its source to where it empties into the China Sea over here at Shanghai. Now Wuchang, where you will be, is about six hundred miles in from the coast and also about six hundred miles north of Hong Kong, so you will be right in the middle!" His pointer flicked from the source of the Yangtze in Tibet to the far west on the map, over to Shanghai on the far eastern edge, then whisked back and forth between Shanghai and Wuchang, and Wuchang and Canton, in a series of swishes and taps.

"Lots of little rivers, about seven hundred or so, flow into the Yangtze. It passes through tall mountains and low-lying areas," he continued. "The watershed of the river is almost seven hundred square miles! Millions and millions of people depend on the river for fish and crops and transportation." He turned with something of a flourish and found her twining a pencil into one of her long ringlets. It occurred to him that his diminutive guest did not quite share his enthusiasm for geographical wonders.

"Miss Polly, you will be living right here in a place marked Wuhan. Wuhan is really three cities. Across the river is Hankow, a much larger city than Wuchang, and down here is Hanyang. And here is Wuchang. I know you will like it there – there are other children your age at the compound where you'll live, and lots of little Chinese girls to make friends with at St. Hilda's School."

Not entirely satisfied, Polly asked how they'd get there. Would they take a boat up the Yangtze?

"My goodness, no. Not from here. As I said, the Yangtze flows to the east, to Shanghai, which is way up the coast. No, my dear, you will board a train and change trains in Canton – here," the pointer was out again, tapping Canton, just north of Hong Kong. "Here you will take a train – a very old train that you will be on for about two-and-a-half days – and then you'll be in your new home, here!"

They were interrupted by Ma just as the pointer slapped Wuchang once again. "There you are!" she said. "We were worried! Come on now, we're almost ready to go. Daddy and Patty are waiting. You mustn't bother Dr. Harth." She apologized to Dr. Harth and he apologized to her, and in the midst of all the apologies, Polly told Ma that they were going to go on a long train to a long river that shed water over millions of Chinese. The train was very, very old, she explained – maybe as old as Dr. Harth!

The train was indeed very old. Most of the railways had been financed through foreign loans during the late colonial period, and the effort to pay off the loans diverted money from upkeep or new equipment. By the time our family entered China, the rail system and trains were verging on obsolescence, but they did run – if often on a fluctuating, unpredictable schedule. Like almost all of the railways, the Canton-Wuhan line had only one track, so one train had to wait on side tracks for an oncoming train to pass, slowing things further. Automobiles were almost non-existent. The primitive roads were designed for foot traffic and animal-drawn carts. Even if one could have driven a car, there were no gas stations or mechanics in the countryside.

As they left Canton, the vast rural landscape stretched out to the horizon in the tropical greens and milky browns of endless rice paddies and terraced fields, dotted by tiny figures and beasts of burden bending to their work. It seemed a world at once primitive and pre-industrial, and yet graceful, enduring, and immutable, resting as it did on thousands of years of an intricate and complex culture. The train was crowded and the days were long, but as they chugged past the flatlands into deep valleys and mountain gorges, past broad rivers and still lakes, past the curving upsweep of tiled-roof temples and pagodas, they felt too much on the brink of something – too charged with the energy of unknown adventure – to think much about mundane issues of comfort.

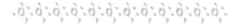

$\mathcal{T}$wo

$\mathcal{I}$N THE EARLY evening of the third day, they arrived, several hours late, at the train depot in Wuchang. A few passengers disembarked. My parents, each carrying one of the girls, followed them onto the worn wooden planks of the nearly deserted platform. Their fellow passengers quickly set off on foot down the dusky dirt road leading away from the station. Several empty rickshaws were lined up in front of the platform. The ticket window was empty, but they could hear a few voices behind the grill. Steam from the engine rose around their legs as they squinted through damp fingers of twilight for other signs of life.

Beyond the station, the low buildings, warehouses, stone walls, and gates of Wuchang huddled together in varying shades of gray, like an old, out-of-focus photograph. Nearby, the crippled hulk of a bombed-out building cropped up in dark relief against the violet sky, silent testament to Japanese air strikes during the war. To the left, the hard-packed dirt road meandered out toward a stretch of open countryside. There didn't seem to be many trees. The gathering darkness was punctuated by embers from a number of open cook fires along the road. They could make out the sounds of laughter and low conversation from clusters of dim figures, some squatting, stirring at pots, some standing. The sharp scent of smoking ginger and frying fish snaked toward them and made their mouths water. Their arms slackened, and they let the girls down.

At the other end of the platform, two men unloaded cartons, sacks of mail, and what appeared to be my parents' trunks onto an iron-wheeled flatbed cart. As the cart creaked toward them, a tall, dignified man materialized from a station door, sweeping toward them in a long black robe. They took him for a priest at first. When he drew closer, they saw that the robe, fastened by small frog clasps from its Mandarin collar to the sweep of its hem, was Chinese, as was the man himself. He bowed briefly, apologized for his lone presence, and introduced himself as Er Lao, their cook. Simultaneously startled and relieved, my parents bowed back, not sure if they should extend their hand or follow his lead. My father said, "Hao pu hao?" – a Chinese greeting he felt sure of. Er Lao smiled and bowed again. Using English that was better than my father's Chinese, he explained that, given the unpredictable train schedule, he'd been sent to fetch our family and had several rickshaws waiting to take them and their luggage to the University compound. There they would meet their neighbors, the Camps, and some of the other faculty. Most important, a warm supper was waiting for them.

"Great! We sure could use something to eat," my father told him. "The food we brought with us from Hong Kong is gone. We're starving!"

"I have prepared a pork stew," Er Lao told them. "And I have prepared a lemon pie."

Lemon pie! My father was immediately won over.

Two years later, the sight of Er Lao on that lonely platform and the memory of his lemon pie were perhaps on all of their minds as Er Lao snapped the last of Ma's suitcases shut. Ma stood nearby, holding me in her arms while issuing instructions and cautions to Dad and "Papa" Camp, who were carrying hand luggage down the stairs. As they loaded it into the compound's only truck, which had miraculously shuddered to life that morning, "Mama" Camp hustled Polly and Patty into their coats. My parents made one last check of the house. It was November 17, 1948. I was nine months old and had been running a fever of unknown origin for four days. Under ordinary circumstances my parents would not have dreamed of undertaking such a long trip. But it was no ordinary time, and the circumstances left them no choice.

The civil war between the Nationalists and the Red Army had stepped up considerably during October and November, and many key northern cities had been taken by the Communists. With the North now under Communist control, the way had opened up for their armies to strike Central China. Shanghai and Nanking were considered the next targets. Even if Wuchang was not a military target, a period of unrest, civil upheaval, and privation was expected as the powers shifted. Already conditions in Wuchang were not very palatable. In response to these potential dangers, the

U.S. Consulate had issued an urgent warning to Americans that they must evacuate the area. As this warning was being considered in the foreign community, Bishop Tsang, the Anglican Bishop of Central China, ordered the three American families in the Mission with small children – the Rhodeses, the Rollinses, and the Starratts – to move the mothers and children out until it was safe for them to return. Anyone else in the Mission was also free to evacuate, but no one did. The fathers decided to accompany their families to Hong Kong and then return to the interior.

At first it appeared the mothers and children would have to be evacuated by military plane to Shanghai, and then all the way back to the U.S. This unhappy possibility was replaced on November 14 when they received notice that the British Consul was arranging an evacuation train to Hong Kong. Word was that it had some room on it for a few Americans. They spent the next three frantic days packing and racing around from the U.S. Consulate to the police station and other sites to arrange the necessary visas and police travel passes. The Rollinses weren't able to get their passes in time to make the train, so it was just the Rhodes family who joined ours for the journey – Henry, who worked for the Mission as a history professor at the University, his wife Catherine, and their three children, who were about the same ages as my sisters and I.

Once again, my parents found themselves at the train station in the early evening, but this time awash in a sea of people crowding the platform, piling up luggage, and struggling to get on the train. Dad and Henry Rhodes had to shout to be heard above the clamor as they checked with the conductor about their berths. After much back and forth, they discovered that the quarters for the families were scattered all over the train. So, they boarded and stumbled about in the dark interior until they were able to make enough trades to secure two adjacent four-berth sleeping compartments. Luckily, the compartments were relatively clean and the windows could open.

Climbing back down and weaving their way through the crowd, they were surprised and pleased to find their families in the midst of a large group of well-wishers there to see them off. The women clucked over my sisters, the other children, and me, and were relieved to learn my fever was subsiding with a sulfa drug prescribed by Dr. Reilly, the physician from the Church General Hospital who had delivered me. Olive Tomlin, my godmother and a teacher at St. Hilda's School, suggested that I might be teething.

Ma reviewed the lists of things for Dad to bring back to the Mission from Hong Kong. Olive, afraid hers wouldn't last another winter, wanted some woolen vests and some new union suits. Bishop Tsang wanted five inexpensive forks. Someone else needed typewriter ribbon and sheets of carbon paper. Another needed combs and a toothbrush. It had all been said before and written down, but the words tumbled out again in rushed repetition against the emotion of their imminent departure.

The whistle sounded above the noise, and it was suddenly time to board. Hugs were given all around, and wishes for a safe trip were accompanied by optimistic hopes for a speedy return. Once on the train, food and supplies were passed to the families by outstretched arms from one person to the next, hand over hand, through the open compartment window.

The train slowly pulled out, and people ran along the platform waving.

"Stay safe!" they shouted. "You'll be back in no time!" "Don't worry, we'll take care of the husbands!" "Take care!" And at the last, "We'll miss you! We'll miss you!"

My father described the scene in a letter to friends back in the States:

The whole Mission was on hand to say good-bye, and I can tell you that there is not a finer group of people on the face of the earth. Presents of fruit, etc. kept coming in until we hardly had room to move. It is only in a place like this where we are strangers in a foreign land and all bound together by our common loyalty . . . that one could possibly develop such dear ties with fellow workers over the short period of two years.

Once on their way toward Changsha and Canton, the families arranged one sleeping compartment as a nursery, doubling the children into the available bunks. The other was for the adults who were not watching the children. My fever cleared on that first evening, and everyone settled in for the two-and-a-half-day journey, hoping the train would not be held up by bandits or troops along the way.

The adults fell quiet after a light meal of cold rice and chicken. Henry and my father read by the dim light. The mothers got the children into their bunks. Somewhere deep into the night, Ma heard me fussing, picked me up, and settled herself in a spot by the window with me against her breast. She stared out in a dim, somnolent state, swaying and rocking, rocking and swaying with the motion of the train. In the reach of never-ending blackness that stretched beyond the smudged pane of glass, images of the life she was leaving swam up in front of her. The massive stone buildings of the campus, the rounded moon gates, the lotus pool behind their house that was visible from the girls' sleeping porch. She saw Er Lao's heavy, round key ring swinging rhythmically against his long blue robe. Keys for the house, the closets, the attic, for the little back room where the refrigerator they shared with the Camps stood. How envious everyone had been when they brought in a refrigerator! How proud Er Lao was of his ring of keys!

She closed her eyes and could see him laughing in the kitchen with her as she taught him to make layer cakes and doughnuts, and he taught her to make Eight Precious Chicken, Chinese Pork Ribs, and Wind Pudding with Custard Sauce. She remembered the first time they discussed buying food for the household, just a short week after their arrival. Few activities gave her more pleasure than shopping at a market, and she wanted to go herself, or at the very least, accompany Er Lao. Quickly recognizing the effort at resisting her was useless, he peacefully resigned himself to the idea that she would have to learn for herself. She smiled now at how wrong she'd been. Down they went to town on foot where the Chinese merchants gave her cans of whatever she wanted. She wanted a tin of bacon? A tin of beans? A frown. These were hard to come by and would cost her extra. They were pleased she was willing to bargain, and she was happy to do so. They would check in the back. They would accommodate. In the back of the shop, knowing they had neither beans nor bacon, the merchants pasted new labels on some cans, writing "beans" on one and "bacon" on another. They handed these to her with broad smiles.

Returning to the house with their straw baskets of food,

Er Lao did not raise an eyebrow as she opened the cans. One of corn. One of powdered milk. It didn't take her long to realize that the merchants preferred to deal with a Chinese cook who knew the kuei chu, the "way" of things, the custom. She wouldn't think now of depriving him of his mornings at the market where he and the merchants, other cooks, and friends exchanged gossip and news of the street as they sipped clear tea from thick cups. The things she had learned!

She remembered buying coal. There was no central heating, of course, so they depended on two or three small coal stoves for heat. The first time the man came to the house to sell coal, he explained it was sold by weight. He weighed the sack and took the money and left. Halfway through the sack, my father discovered a hefty stone nestled among the chunks of coal. When the coal man returned, my father complained, and the man laughed to know he had figured this out. Told my father he was very clever, and that this time there would be no stones among the coal. For the second time the coal was weighed and the sack taken to the back of the house. But the coal failed to ignite in the stoves. The coal man returned, delighted that my father had learned that wet coal weighed more than dry. A hint of respect crept into the crinkled folds around the old man's eyes as he nodded and bowed at my father's increasing knowledge.

They had learned much about the kuei chu in two years. They had learned, as well, about the great importance and complexities of "face." One time Dad decided to lose a few of the extra pounds he'd gained eating Er Lao's good cooking. Er Lao seemed indifferent to his efforts, and in fact, had engaged in some dietary sabotage by consistently preparing all Dad's favorite dishes and desserts. Finally, when confronted, Er Lao explained he would have no "face" among the other cooks if they found out Dad was losing weight.

A month or so after they arrived, Er Lao found them an Amah to help with the children and with the household chores that Er Lao considered beneath him. These positions gave work to the Chinese and were expected as a means of spreading the comparative wealth of the Mission among the local people. Er Lao heard of a potential Amah from another cook named Wong Shih Fu, who had heard about a woman in need of work from a friend, Tsai Hoien Sheng. Tsai worked at the hospital, and the woman in question was a relative of his. Tsai was in the awkward position of wanting to find work for her, but knowing he would have no "face" if it became generally known that one of his family was looking for work. So he very quietly asked Wong Shih Fu to help out. And Wong Shih Fu whispered to Er Lao. And so it went.

The Amah was a diminutive young woman in her late twenties who did their laundry and helped them around the house – from my mother's point of view, often helping a bit too much. Soon after she was hired, Ma was shocked to discover Polly and Patty, passive as little dolls, sticking their feet straight out as the Amah put on their shoes and socks. At four and five years old, they were certainly capable of putting on their own shoes and socks, yet there was the Amah bent over their feet like a personal handmaiden! Ma clapped her hands, gave a quick stop to that activity, and scolded the girls for not dressing themselves.

An even more surprising event occurred later that same evening. Dad was in the kitchen near the stove, sitting in the wooden tub they used for bathing. In came the Amah carrying a sponge and pitcher. Ma's eyebrows nearly rose to her hairline. "Whatever are you doing?" she wanted to know.

"I will wash him," the Amah said positively.

"Over my dead body," Ma said to herself. What she said out loud was that such a service was quite unnecessary. With that she reached toward the pitcher and sponge. The Amah held the pitcher back.

"Someone must wash him!" she cried in protest, pointing and gesturing at my father.

"I will manage it," was my mother's steady response. This time she took firm steps toward the Amah, who, perhaps afraid Ma was going to hit her, sidestepped away to the other side of the tub. Ma pursued her, and the Amah began to shriek, to run faster, darting this way and that around the tub. Water sloshed out of the pitcher. The floor became a slippery mess. Hearing the commotion, Er Lao rushed in and joined the dance, trying his best to corner the Amah while shouting at her in Chinese. In the center of it all, my father stood halfway up, but quickly crouched back down, sheepishly aware that he was wearing nothing but soapy water. Finally, Er Lao was able to explain things to the Amah, and as my mother helped to calm and soothe her, the Amah began to appreciate something of the kuei chu of the Starratt household.

She smiled at this memory and saw now that the train was passing through a narrow gorge. She could just make out the side of the mountain. As they curved closer to the towering cliffs, there was an odd rushing noise that turned into an eerie, almost singing sound. She closed her eyes. The mysterious sound washed around her, and in it she began to hear the sweet, high-pitched voices of the children from the School for the Blind, faint at first, then louder. She startled, but then put her head back against the seat and let the memory of her first visit to the school flood over her.

Mrs. Eckhart had ushered their small party into a low dining area where the children stood in neat rows before them. Each child had a white handkerchief pinned to the front of his or her blouse. They were absolutely still while the guests seated themselves. Then Mrs. Eckhart gave a signal, and their voices joined in unison, taking those listening to a separate place. They sang a Chinese song and several familiar Anglican children's hymns in Chinese. A single hand drum kept the rhythm, and they finished in English with the rousing, "In Christ there is no-oh East or West, in him no South or-r North, but one great fel-low-ship of love, Through-ou-out the whole wide earth. . . . Join hands, then, brothers of the faith, What ere your race may be! Who serves my Father as a son, is surely kin to me."

"No, no East or West," Ma thought, tapping the tune with her toes, "indeed, no East or West."

At the end of the singing, they performed a little dance to cymbal and gong. Never missing a step, they wound around each other in a simple chain, braids straight as arrows down their backs, their unseeing eyes masked by the purposeful expressions on their round faces. When their concert was over, they bowed deeply from the waist, barely able to contain their delight in the hearty applause, some clapping along with everyone else. They bowed again and were led by their teachers to meet the guests. When they got to Polly and Patty, the blind children gathered around, reaching toward them. Remarkably, without betraying the slightest discomfort of mind or body, the girls allowed the little fingers to patter over their noses, eyelashes, brows, and mouths and to wind in and out of their long ringlets. Then the older children led the two little girls off hand-in-hand as their teacher guided them toward the cakes and candied ginger on the table. Young as they were, it was as if Polly and Patty knew they'd been given a great gift in the presence of these brave children – children protected by the Mission from the life of begging so often accorded the infirm by families too poor to support them, children who found joy among the ashes, who by so doing, elevated all those in their presence.

The words "one great fellowship of love" stayed with her as she rested her eyes. That is what the Mission was to her, to both of them. A church, she thought, like St. Anne's back home, was also a place of fellowship, but very different. There, the minister is alone among his congregation, who see him as their leader, but also keep watch over him as their employee. He answers to God certainly, and to the bishop, but also to the congregation who usually have a variety of opinions about how things should be done – from the color of the rugs in the chancel, to the importance of the choir, to the need to re-paint the rectory. At the Mission, they all served as equals, tightly connected as volunteers in a foreign land, each with his own opinion and inner spiritual life, certainly, but each bound to the other in a common vision that was ever-present and almost always more prominent than the petty concerns that naturally arise in such close quarters.

A constant round of scheduled and spontaneous gatherings supported the sense of family, as did the shared sense of purpose toward the community and the students. Huachung was a Christian university, made up of Chinese and foreign faculty, some British and some American. The foreign community was supported by the Anglican Mission. There were some

Methodists and a Catholic or two on the compound, but almost everyone else was Anglican, or Episcopalian, as the Anglican Church is called in America. Many members of the Mission were lay workers – professors at the University, teachers at the School for the Blind, and at the two middle schools, St. Hilda's for girls and the Boon School for boys. A few were doctors and nurses at the hospital, the clinic, and the baby clinic. Others, like my father, were clergy, as well as professors, and were responsible for services for the churches and the chapel. Nearly everyone, it seemed, including the professional women and some of the wives, gave chapel talks at the early morning and evening services.

They lived in divided houses or in apartments on either the University or the hospital compound. Their salaries were meager. They put up with damp, cold winters followed by unbearably hot, humid summers, with ash and soot from coal stoves, and with the threat of diseases like cholera, dysentery, and the ever-present tuberculosis. They learned to live with the occasional visit of rats and with strange flying insects in their houses. They made do without many of the conveniences that were common in their home countries – central heating, telephones, cars, and little things like bottled milk, pipe cleaners, peanut butter and talcum powder. As often as not, they turned making do into having fun. They crafted their Christmas decorations out of paper and paste and tin can lids and whatever else was at hand. They recycled old cards for birthdays and holidays and hand-delivered them when stamps were too costly to waste. They shared the contents of "missionary barrels," those parcels from various church groups and ladies' auxiliaries back home containing such things as ten-cent mysteries, used toys (sometimes broken, sometimes not), old clothes, periodicals, and once a second-hand brown suit which, after a bit of tailoring, became my father's best suit. There was always excitement when a package came from family or friends back home. Most contained foodstuffs – tins of sardines, cocoa, baking powder, marmalade, butter, bacon, and coffee; packs of cards; and puzzles. Sometimes there were old *Time* magazines, talcum, tooth powder, shoelaces, and used baby blankets and quilts. What one family might not use was shared with another.

Like any family, they shared hard times and good ones. There were plenty of differing opinions, not so much on politics, but often on religion. Those with a liberal interpretation of Christianity rankled the conservatives, and vice versa. Some were dogmatic, but the search for meaning, both spiritual and intellectual, encouraged discussion. Students learned through lively debate among their professors that differences did not have to spell discord. There were regularly scheduled meetings of the philosophy club where the topics ranged from Plato to geopolitics. At meetings of the "Theologs," the theological students and faculty took on topics such as neorealism and nominalism. And there were often nights of "stump the teachers," when students could test the wits of a panel of professors. Never again did my father encounter students as dedicated to truth or as eager to learn as his Chinese students at Huachung.

On Friday nights, professors and clergy hosted ten to fifteen student members of the S.K.H. in their homes for Fellowship meetings. S.K.H. stood for Sheng Kung Huei, which translates literally into "Holy Togetherness Church," the term given to the Anglican Church in China. Ma recalled how shy and stiff the male and female students were at first, sitting straight as ramrods in their chairs at the house, barely touching the cakes and custards, barely speaking a word. One day Dad devised some games for a dart board he'd made to break the ice. The giggles and laughter opened the way, and from that point on, serious discussion about what Christianity could do to meet the needs of contemporary Chinese young people was sandwiched between the fun and games. The students even asked if they could bring their friends. Dad had to think up more games. He relied heavily on the campfire games he'd learned as a counselor at Camp O-AT-KA, the Episcopal boys camp in Maine where he had decided to enter the ministry. Eventually his S.K.H. Fellowship nights proved so popular that Bishop Tsang asked him to write a game book manual in Chinese for youth leaders. He finished it the summer before he left Wuchang for good.

There was also a steady round of get-togethers among the Mission family. Someone was always inviting a group in for dinner, followed by cards and parlor games. Someone was always having tea in the afternoons or having a lecture series. There were sing-alongs, hymn-sings, quartets, and gramophone nights. They put on plays and had dress-up nights. There were ongoing chess championships. And there were long evenings spent on the grass outside their homes as the sunset faded to soft moonlight, and evenings filled with quiet conversation and time to think.

Ma, who had so worried about the conditions in a foreign land, had found that the conditions in Wuchang were the last thing on her mind as the train took her away from what had so quickly become "home." She remembered Mama and Papa

Camp, who had been together in China for over forty years, saying to her during that first month that she would soon find herself so grounded in the Mission, so deeply rooted, that she would not want to leave when their ten years was up.

How right they had been! She had adjusted quickly, just as many years before as a small child she had adjusted to the ways of America on the streets of Boston when her family had emigrated from the Ukraine. She had embraced every aspect of the New World – the settlement house, the shops, the school, the church. She became the lawyer and diplomat for the family, an interpreter between the old ways and the new. When she was twelve, her family moved from their urban enclave to a farm in the small town of Norwell where she became a mother's helper to a Dr. Whitmore and his family. She volunteered to take on more and more duties, stoking the furnace early in the mornings, preparing breakfast for the family before she went to school. When she decided to attend nursing school, they, in their gratitude, bought her a car so she could get to and from Boston. Nursing turned out to be a natural extension of her skills and her desire to help others.

China was a place where she felt she could also serve, and so the transition had not proven nearly as arduous as she had envisioned. My father was well aware of her adaptability, aware, too, of her discomfort with uncertainty. Several months into their separation, while she and we children were refugees in Hong Kong, he would write:

. . . your last three letters indicate that you really feel that you have roots right here in Wuchang and you want to stay and see the job through. It all reminds me of a conversation, which we had in the dim

past when you first realized that I was serious about wanting to go to China. I told you then that I'd bet that once you got adjusted to it you wouldn't want to leave – even if we were living in a mud hut! Now with good reasons to throw in the sponge and return to "God's Country," you still write about looking forward to seeing our "home" on the compound again. It is almost as if the Chinese couldn't throw you out of their country even though they have tried.

Of course I know just as well as you that it is not simply a love for the place that holds you here. There's a satisfying job to do, and there are wonderful people to work with, and there is the determination to see the thing through. But even so, such things would not help very much if you did not have a natural genius for making a real home wherever you may be. . . . I suppose that from that point of view, you are an ideal Missionary's wife. . . . So, chalk up another star in your crown of virtues while I hum a Te Deum of thanksgiving for having captured such a wonderful woman for my mate.

All she knew as she put me back down in the train that night was that she was already missing the place she called "home," their lovely two-story stone house, attached to the Camp's, with their common garden, the willow tree, the lotus pool, the upstairs view of the fields beyond the stone walls of the campus, the proximity of all those on the compound. Most of all, of course, she would miss her husband, their long evening strolls, their romantic encounters on the sleeping porch – especially the previous spring, which nine months later had produced the infant she had just put down. The threads of life that they had woven together were much on her mind as she slipped into the narrow space on the bunk next to Dad.

But she was sure to be back as soon as life in China quieted down again, perhaps in a month or two, she told herself. For now she would have the one room to share with the children. As the rhythm of the train lulled her to sleep, her thoughts drifted toward making a new, if temporary, home.

$\mathscr{T}hree$

$\mathscr{D}$AD STRAINED TO get up, stiff from kneeling over the wooden slats of the crib he was assembling. Several busy days had passed since their arrival at the Church Guest House in Hong Kong.

"Well," he said, "guess that about does it. I think we can set it upright now."

Together my parents turned the small crib over and set it next to Ma's iron bed. They put the mattress in and stood back from their labors. Seconds later, the back left leg wobbled, made a kind of creaking noise, and gently bent inward. The crib listed to the left for a moment until the right leg followed suit, and slowly the crib sat itself down like some spindly animal, its two rear legs neatly folded. My father, never the expert in home repairs, wordlessly handed Ma the screwdriver and held the crib while she applied the tool to the errant screws.

This bit of re-assembling done, they surveyed the completed quarters. There were two chairs, Ma's bed, a cot for each girl, and woven straw sleeping mats stored underneath the beds for the hot weather that would come. There was one bureau and two large trunks stuffed with clothes, linens, and a few favored possessions. The bathroom was down the hall; the dining hall, on the first floor. With my crib our room was tight, but from its vantage point on the second story there was a good view of Victoria Park. More than that, it was clean and safe – and we were lucky to have it.

The Guest House was quite full. There were some Chinese students and many British and American missionaries. A few, like us, were in a wait-and-see mode, but the vast majority were on their way out of China for good. Many questioned the sanity of going back in, but Dad and Henry Rhodes were determined to continue their work in Wuchang. They hoped that conditions in their area would soon clear and that they could return to Hong Kong to retrieve their wives and children during the term break in February.

In the course of their week in Hong Kong, my parents had made all the arrangements for what they hoped would be a brief sojourn. Dad had set up a small kerosene stove to keep us warm. With Dr. Harth's directions they'd made their way through the city of Victoria by trolley and on foot, up and down the many stone steps that connected the upper streets to those below, buying provisions for themselves and their friends in Wuchang. Ma had absolutely no sense of direction. To help her find her way back to the Guest House in future excursions, Dad made maps and repeatedly pointed out major landmarks.

They both agreed that it was strange to be back in British-owned Hong Kong after so long a time in the heart of

China. As Dad put it several weeks later in a letter to friends back in Lincoln, Massachusetts:

I can't really describe to you what it felt like to arrive in Hong Kong . . . when we stepped off the train to be greeted by friendly, courteous, trustworthy policemen, to see clean, wide, well-paved and well-lighted streets, to hear people all around speaking English again; well, I could have knelt down and kissed the ground. . . . I never hope to meet any finer friends than my Chinese friends in Wuchang, and I am ready to do anything I can to help them — but home is still home and one can never really forget it.

Setting up the crib was the last of their tasks before his scheduled departure the following day. As Ma pulled a mirror from a trunk and set it on the bureau, Dad asked, "Think you can manage here for a month or so – in one room like this?"

"Oh, we'll be fine. The girls have built-in playmates with the Rhodes and Stevens children. It won't be long. We'll make do," Ma reassured him.

She faced the mirror and raised her hands to the ribbon that had held her hair in place while working on the crib. She saw Dad move toward her in the reflection as she untied the bow. He caught her wrist quickly, then slowly slipped the ribbon out of her hair into his upturned palm. Their gaze held in the reflection until he turned her into his arms and held her there in the stillness of the afternoon, held her tight against their unspoken fears, held her in wordless embrace.

The ribbon was in his pocket the next day as he and Henry made their farewells. They admonished the older children to help their mothers with the babies, kissed their wives, and headed off in a taxi to the station. After an uneventful several days on the train, they arrived back in Wuchang on December 1. Dad greeted Er Lao, shaved and ate, then went immediately to his little study. It was cold and damp. A north wind buffeted the house and sent a chill right through him. He moved the typing table next to the little coal stove, put on his long johns, or "longies," as he called them, a second sweater, his padded "ee-fu" jacket, and the fingerless gloves Ma had knit for him. Then he scrolled a thin sheet of paper into the typewriter:

Dearest Anne,

How can I tell you what it felt like to come into this bare and oh so quiet house this morning! I'm sure that if it were not against the masculine "kuei chu," I would have just sat down and wept. I can't tell you how much I miss my four darlings, and I have looked longingly at my new picture of you all at least a dozen times since I left you. . . . Really Anne, you can't imagine what it is like without you here. I find it hard to get my mind on the things I have to do as I keep remembering your face, and Polly and Patty and that darling, sweet little Penny. . . .

Thus began the first of the daily letters he would write to my mother during their separation, a separation played out against the backdrop of war, an uncertain future, devotion to his work, and a constant and acute longing for his family. He numbered the letters and saved the carbons. When the postal service wasn't running, he gave packets of letters to be hand-delivered by anyone he knew bound for Hong Kong. When mail was not an option, he sent brief telegrams at exorbitant fees to let us know about the situation and the dimming possibility of our return.

Later that evening he, Er Lao, and a young man named Philip Stowe, who taught at the Boon Middle School, huddled around the radio. They fiddled with the dial, trying to pull in the Armed Services station from Manila against the intermittent whistles and static crackling over the airwaves. Although they were in the heart of Central China, it was difficult to get an accurate reading on the war going on around them. The local Chinese newspapers were controlled by the Nationalists and were severely censored. Radio reports from the Nationalists and the Communists routinely contradicted each other. The occasional *Voice of America* broadcasts suffered from lack of immediate contact with the action. Thus, a report was considered a rumor unless it was repeated from several sources over several days. But it was often on rumor that they had to depend.

The news on the radio that evening was that Hsuchow, a key city on the Yangtze Delta, was lost to the Communists. There was fighting now just fifty miles from the Nationalist capital of Nanking, and there was a mad exodus from the city. Not surprisingly, the next day the Nationalists denied the report about Nanking and claimed that Hsuchow was an unimportant and insignificant city.

The crucial issue for the future, as seen by those in the Anglican Mission in Wuchang and Hankow, was not so much who won the war, as when it would end and the nature of the peace to follow. Would they be allowed to stay in China? Would they be allowed to carry on their work, even if under some level of restriction and privation? For those with small children, would the sacrifices be too great for the safety and health of their families?

Although they had joined forces to oust the Japanese

from China during World War II, Mao Tse-tung, head of the Communist forces, or Red Army, and Chiang Kai-shek, head of the Nationalist government and the Kuomintang army, were bitter enemies. In most areas under Nationalist control, there were gross mismanagement, outright corruption, and diversion of public funds and foreign aid into private accounts. In a loose alliance with local warlords, the plight of the peasant and coolie – disenfranchised, impotent, and mired in poverty – continued as it had for centuries. Despite this, the Nationalist government was bolstered by U.S. aid as the hope of democracy and the line of defense against the spread of Communism. The Chinese Communists saw themselves in a class struggle as leaders of a peasant revolt. They did not promise democracy, but they promised change and a square meal in the belly. Horrible atrocities and reprisals were being committed during the long civil war by both sides, and all of China suffered.

A Nationalist victory would pretty much ensure that Mission work would continue. But it seemed doubtful that the Nationalists could win the war, and many privately feared for China if they did. Inflation was rampant. Thousands were being turned out of their homes, and thousands more were starving. The Nationalist regime had done nothing and had no plan to ease the situation. The Kuomintang army was largely demoralized and uncertain of its cause. Many battles for outlying areas were concluded following a pre-arranged plan. A few perfunctory shots would be fired, and then the Kuomintang troops would sell their American-made weapons to the Communists and either join them or simply walk home. Desertions were so frequent in the Kuomintang that on long marches foot soldiers were tied one to the other with looping ropes around their necks to prevent them from running off. Even the officer corps was not immune. High-ranking military leaders had been told by the government that their wives and families had been transported to Nanking, Shanghai, and Taiwan "for their safety." But everyone knew the families were being held hostage as insurance against officer defections. It was rumored that independent warlords, like Pai Chung Hsi who ruled the Wuhan area, were considering separate negotiations with the Red Army. Yet, in many places the Nationalists held out much longer than anyone expected, so the outcome remained unknown.

A Communist victory left the future much more uncertain, but not without hope. As naive as it may sound now, the idea that foreigners might be tolerated and that Mission work could continue under Communist rule was not unfounded. Although some Missions had been burned and looted, it was not clear whether the damage had been done by Communist soldiers or by bandits. News on the street from cities like Kaifeng, now in Communist hands, suggested that academic and religious freedoms were being maintained, if only temporarily. Equally important, the Missions in those areas were still allowed to receive funds from their Mission Boards abroad. It was also rumored that foreigners, even Americans, were being tolerated. American nationals were especially vulnerable if the Communists won. Not only was the U.S. backing Chiang, but it was very unlikely that the U.S. would ever recognize a Communist state in China.

Opinions – about the future, who might win, and what their victory might mean – varied from morning to afternoon, depending on the latest rumor. Dr. Wei, ever the optimist, did a great deal to keep up the morale of his University staff with hopes of an early negotiated peace. However, nine days into December, Bishop Tsang sent word across the river from Hankow that he wanted to meet with all thirty-five foreign members of the Mission four days hence.

Speculation about the purpose of the meeting reverberated throughout the compound. No one knew exactly what the bishop had in mind. His insistence on the presence of every foreigner fueled nervous guesses that the Episcopal Church Missions House in New York (the Mission Board that paid their salaries and governed their activities) had sent a directive that they had to get out. Mama Camp summed up the feelings of most when she said that the Mission Board was probably thinking, "Those dear people in Hankow and Wuchang are very brave, and we love them all, but if they haven't sense enough to take care of themselves, it is up to us to see that they are moved to safety."

On December 13, my father and the others headed out of the compound for Hankow. Enveloped in a cold, wintry afternoon mist, they walked to the river landing along the back roads, past the public washing pools and rows of flimsy lean-tos erected by the local poor and by homeless refugees. They boarded what my father called the "broken-down launch that passes for a ferry" and slowly crossed the Yangtze against the wind. Once in Hankow, they made their way through crowded streets to the bishop's house in what had now become a driving rain.

When they arrived, Bishop Tsang greeted them warmly in the foyer as they removed their wet coats and tried to shake off the cold. He ushered them into the front room where the lamplight cast a soft glow on the dark rosewood paneling. They were grateful for the cups of hot tea passed around as they found a place to sit among the chairs and sofas.

They settled down quickly after exchanging greetings with the Hankow members of the Mission. There was not a person in the room who did not know that the bishop had recently risked his life checking on distant out-stations, traveling through country infested by bandits and beyond the reach of the authorities on either side of the civil war. They were more than anxious to hear what he had to say.

He began the meeting by stating that it appeared that they were the only people in the entire Mission still at their stations. The Central Theological School in Shanghai and other Anglican schools had closed. Thousands were fleeing from Nanking, including all those connected to Missions there. In Changsha, a city less than two hundred miles to the southwest, foreign members of the great Yale-in-China Mission, along with all other foreigners, had been pulled out by U.S. military planes. He reported that conditions downriver must have become quite bad to have brought about the general exodus that was taking place in Central China. The purpose of the meeting, he said, was to give every individual a chance to have his say about what they should do in the present crisis. First, however, he wanted to offer a prayer.

Everyone settled their cups on nearby tables or the floor, and the room grew quiet and then silent. A violent gust of wind rattled the tall windows, hurling a burst of rain like a spray of bullets against the glass panes. Bishop Tsang, eyes closed, stood motionless. Then, in a soft voice that filled the room, he said, "Dear Lord, look favorably upon us, and enter our hearts. Allow each person here to be so guided by the Holy Spirit that they may have the courage to express what they honestly feel should be done in our situation. Amen."

With that, he turned to those assembled and waited. Deaconess Kent, in a shadowed corner of the room, was the first to speak. With some effort she raised herself out of her high-backed, padded chair, and in a thin but steady voice she said, "China is my home." She leaned on the chair in front of her and continued, "I have given all my life to these people. My one sadness, now that I am old, is facing the fact that the Mission Board will call me back to the States for good. So, if I am killed, it will only be the fulfillment of my wishes, for I am content to die here." With that, she sat down.

Mama Camp spoke up next. "I have refugeed from my station four times during periods of war and unrest, and I wish that this time I could say that I would leave now when I can go in peace and take a few things with me. But this time is like all other times. We have a job to do, and we can't leave so long as there is any way to carry on. I am staying with my husband, come what may." Papa Camp reached over and took her hand.

Mother Johanna from the Episcopalian Convent said that she and the sisters would carry on at the orphanage so long as they would be permitted to do so. "And if that privilege is taken away," she said, "we will stay and serve our people in prayer."

And so it went around the room. One after another, without exception, each man and woman voiced his determination to stay on the job. They said they were serving the church, not any one group or race. Their attitude toward their new rulers, whoever they might be, was that they, too, were God's children to whom they owed the same duties of love and service that they owed the rest of their Chinese friends. They agreed that the decision to stay was their own responsibility and was made knowing full well the dangers involved – a possible battle and certainly the period of anarchy that would precede any change in government. We are here, they said, to serve the Chinese people, and we see no reason to abandon them in time of need. They hoped to convince the new rulers that they were not agents of foreign imperialism. They concluded that no political group, however powerful, can long endure if it is not motivated by a loving goodwill toward all men. "Surely," my father added, "there are enough people on the earth who are trying to solve the world's problems by means of power politics. One can hardly blame the few of us who are here in the middle of China trying to meet antagonism in another way."

Someone else said, "If conditions become so bad that families cannot live here and there is no foreseeable hope of improvement, then they may have to withdraw as family units." Everyone agreed that those with dependent children had an obligation to their families which must be fulfilled.

On the return trip across the river that evening, Dad stood near the bow of the sputtering launch, watching heavy drops of rain splash against the dark, churned-up waters of the Yangtze. Drop after drop held him mesmerized until he lifted his eyes and saw the lights and lanterns of Wuchang glinting on the approaching shore. Late that night he shared his feelings in a letter to friends in New England:

These are not extraordinary people. They are simply everyday folk who have given their lives in a way that really counts. Yet that loyalty of theirs has a bigness about it – a bigness that makes you feel

that they are more than thirty-five people in the center of a vast coun-
try and hundreds of miles from the nearest place of refuge. . . . And
then it came to me what it was that made it seem so big. In the loyal-
ty of those few missionaries is the very power of God – the power that
is not found in force or armies or atom bombs or money or any other
thing except in the loving hearts of men and women who have offered
all they have and all they are. . . . The power of those thirty-five peo-
ple is indeed a big power, and the future of China and the hope of the
world rests finally in that kind of power, and that kind alone. There is
only one thing that truly abides, and that is love.

It rained on and off for most of December and got cold-
er, yet spirits remained buoyed, and the Mission got back to
the work at hand. They raised funds amongst themselves to
help support the baby clinic and the project to teach illiterate
servants to read. Classes continued at the University, as did
the regular round of fellowship meetings and clubs.

Snow flew toward the end of the month. Dad bundled
more sweaters under his linen cassock for the earliest morning services at which only a few stragglers appeared in heavy
coats and padded jackets. Despite his fingerless gloves, he
found he sometimes had to soak his hands in warm water
before attempting to type notes for his thesis, lectures, ser-
mons, and letters. Several of his students from distant towns
returned home and then came back again when it appeared
there would be no fighting near Wuchang for several
months. Er Lao wasn't worried about the fighting, having
heard a rumor from a merchant in town that the Marines
were going to protect Shanghai. "There is no reason the
United States Marines could not march into the University

and set up a gun or two at each gate," he said. "Then the Shih m'ong [the title Er Lao used for my mother] will be back in business here!"

Philip Stowe moved in and brought a most welcome extra stove with him. He, Dad, and Er Lao set up a "bachelor's quarters" in the house. The lights failed on and off, so Dad set up the big oil lamp on a table where he and Philip could read or play chess in the evenings. The house cat had kittens and ran off a week later. Dad asked Ma to tell Polly that Er Lao was being a good mother to abandoned kittens and that two of them seemed to say "Patty" when they cried. "I think those two must be the two that Polly wants to give to Patty when they come back to Wuchang," he wrote.

He went twice a day to the post box, eagerly anticipating a letter from Ma, but none came. He had no idea if she was receiving his letters until he finally got a telegram from her saying "letters arriving." He and Henry figured the only explanation for the letter holdup was that mail was being censored by the Nationalists. When Dad finally received his first letter from her, around the 20th of December, he held it as if it were gold, read it and re-read it many times over. In her broad, curling script, she wrote that Polly and Patty were enrolled in the King George V School just down the street, that she had many friends, had seen *Hamlet* in a movie theater, was taking the children to Victoria Park every afternoon, and that, despite the fact that all was well, she could not wait to return to him in Wuchang.

Despite his many requests, she never dated her letters, but she did adopt his letter numbering system which helped them both know when letters did not get through. When letters did get through, he sometimes had trouble deciphering her handwriting. With some amusement he wrote:

I received your number 3 letter today. Some of it was a bit illegible. For example, I haven't yet figured out the meaning of the enclosed bit which I cut out from the end of the letter. The "Love from us all" is clear enough, but what are the words after that? It looks like "Kur Pork Horse" Or is it "Two turk hover?" But, perhaps, after all, what you meant to write were the simple words, "Kur herk hives." If so, I'm afraid you will have to translate the meaning for me. I shall be looking forward to finding out what you meant – that is if you can figure it out yourself!

As Christmas approached, the Mission drew together even more as a family. They planned a performance of the *Messiah*, with many of those on the compound participating. Buying gifts all around was out of the question, so they each drew the name of one person to whom they were to give a gift, which could either be something they owned or something that would cost no more than ten cents U.S. Dad was to distribute the gifts in a makeshift Santa suit made by Mrs. Constantine, and he wrote a ballad for the occasion that included each person's name. There were extra services and parties for the student fellowship groups.

But the closer it got to Christmas, the more Dad longed for his own family. He was suddenly overcome during supper one night when he and Er Lao heard an orchestra on the radio playing, "I'm Dreaming of a White Christmas." That night he wrote to Ma:

Aye Yah! How can one sing "Silent Night, Holy Night" this

*Christmas? Oh, how I wish you were going to be here, and how I some-
times wish we were going to be home in New England. . . . This evening,
I wanted to chuck the whole thing and join you for a trip home on the
first boat available. I feel so lonely and cold and hopeless. Probably it
has been our time here together that has done it – but whatever the
cause I am no longer the fellow who could go it alone without too much
unhappiness. Now my life is bound up in the four of you, and the whole
flavor of living has gone bad because my thoughts and hopes and
dreams are all with you. Never again will I complain about anyone in
my family interrupting my work. What I would give to have Polly or
Patty come running in with a hug and a kiss, or to hear Penny crying
for attention in the next room, or to have you stop in to tell me the latest bit of gossip. . . . Kiss the girls for me and be sure to hold my picture in front of Penny a few times every day so that she will remember
who I am. How I long to see you all! Goodnight, my four darlings. . . .*

That Christmas was not easy in Hong Kong either. Ma
took the girls and me to the Cathedral for the midnight service on Christmas Eve. The church was overflowing with
European and American refugees from the mainland, many
of whom carried tales of horror, and all of whom were overcome with a mixture of relief for the safe refuge of Hong
Kong and grief at all they had left behind – dear friends, the
lives they had made there. The lights dimmed at the end of
the service, and in the darkness all around them, the congregation fell to their knees. In silence they clasped hands in
prayer or held hands with one another and looked toward the
altar, illuminated in a blaze of candlelight flame flickering and
reflecting off the outstretched arms of the brass cross at its
center. The soft opening chords of "Silent Night, Holy Night"

began on the organ. In faint voices the congregation joined in. Sobs were audible, and voices broke. Ma could only whisper the words as the strains of that beautiful hymn played quietly to conclusion.

Four

A PALE LIGHT still hung in the sky, yet it was almost 5:30. "Spring trying to get through," my father thought, looking out the arched window of the classroom toward Stokes Hall. It was the end of February. Behind him, heads bent over their work, his students scratched out answers to their regular Wednesday quiz. He had just finished his lecture on the intersections between Taoism and Christianity with some words about an early Christian scholar. "The point is this," Dad explained. "Men like Clement of Alexandria recognized the fact that there is a supreme revelation of the divine in the life of Jesus, but that the revelation is not limited to him alone. Wherever a sincere mind is seeking the truth, there God waits to meet the seeker."

He was glad the lecture was over. He was very tired, having just returned from a two-week visit to Hong Kong. At the end of the winter term, he and Henry had taken the opportunity to see the families while it was still safe enough to travel. But everyone had to agree that it was not yet safe enough to bring the families back in. Bishop Tsang had sent a telegram to that effect at the end of their two weeks, and that had settled the matter.

He looked at his watch again just as the heavy gong in the chapel sounded the half-hour.

"Time," he said to the rows of dark heads. Pens dropped promptly. The students filed up to his desk and placed their papers in a neat stack on the blotter. Cheerful chatter swelled briefly in the hall, fading again as the last of the students went out through the main entrance.

Dad stuffed the papers into his briefcase. Then, in the quiet of the empty building, he was drawn back to the stone casement. Leaning against it, watching the light drain from the sky, he thought about the chapel talk he was to give that evening. His topic was faith. He planned to say that while faith could mean acceptance of a body of doctrine, spiritual faith was not "blind faith" in doctrine and creed, but rather a loving trust in the source of the highest values one knows. "Faith," he decided to say, "is more than rites and piety; it is alive with power."

Tinkling sounds of laughter broke into his reflections. Below him, a little snake of lights was weaving its way along the broad path toward the East Gate. He saw it was the kindergarten and first grade children, each carrying a lantern on a stick, led by their teachers in some special celebration. His lofty thoughts bobbled away with the lantern lights as he watched the tiny procession.

"Excuse me," someone behind him said.

Startled, he looked across the gathering gloom of the classroom and made out Yan Chiao Ming in the doorway.

Yan was a student whom he was teaching in a private tutorial. "Come in, come in, Yan," he said. Yan entered, trailed by two other boys. Dad recognized one of the boys, Li Shan To, from another class. The other, he thought, may have visited Fellowship Group once or twice.

Yan bowed and introduced the boys. My father bowed to each in return. Yan explained that the boys wanted to be baptized. Yan himself had been baptized the previous year and had chosen the name Alfred C. M. Yan for his baptismal name.

"Well," Dad said, "that's a serious decision. Perhaps we can set up a time to discuss it." Privately, he was surprised and pleased. Although he was not bent on converting students to Christianity, he was heartened that his students took their spiritual lives seriously.

"We are impressed with your philosophy," Li Shan To said. "My father had his doubts about my coming to Huachung because it was connected to the Anglican Mission. When he was a boy, missionaries passed through our village and urged him and his friends to become Christians because then they would not have to waste money buying incense and other objects for worshipping at the temples. Please excuse me, but my father was offended," he said.

"I don't blame him," Dad responded. "Imagine! Join the Christian faith because it is cheaper! Of all the rot!" He shook his head.

"Yes. Just so. But we have seen real faith here, not superstition. Our foreign teachers here have not run off when others have," Li continued. "You talk of many paths to peace. We wish to follow yours."

They made plans to meet the following day, left the building, pulling the heavy doors shut behind them, and parted ways under the long, dark shadow of a willow, pale hints of green visible on its graceful boughs. The little lantern lights were at the far end of the courtyard, coming his way. My parents' dear friend Olive Tomlin was leading them.

"Alfred!" she said when their paths crossed. "How good to see you! I meant to stop in today to find out how the trip to Hong Kong was. How is Anne? How are the girls and my goddaughter, Penny?"

The little children clustered around them, lanterns bobbing. "How is Pao Li? How is Pao Mei? Are they back yet?" several little voices asked in Chinese. Pao Li, Precious Jasmine, was Polly's Chinese name. Patty's was Pao Mei, Precious Beauty. My mother's name was Pao An, Precious Peace.

"What about baby sister?" a tiny girl wanted to know. "Is she with them far away?"

"Yes," my father answered. "She is with them. Dr. Wei gave her a Chinese name, the other day. It's Pao Ngai."

"Ahhh," they said.

"Pao Ngai, Precious Love," Olive repeated to her charges.

"Do come over after your chapel talk, Alfred," she said, turning again to my father. "I want all the news."

Later that evening, he and Olive shared a pot of green tea across the bright yellow oil cloth on her kitchen table. "Tell me everything," Olive said.

Dad lit a cigarette and handed one to Olive. "Got these in Hong Kong at a fraction of the price" he said. "Things are good there. Anne has made quite a few friends and is managing well. Of course, she's anxious to return. The room is awfully small, bathroom down the hall, and so on, and the place is getting really crowded. The biggest problem for her right now is that Penny is a night owl, and there's no way to train her out of it. It's too crowded and the walls are too thin to let her cry at night, so the first little whimper and she gets picked up – which she thinks is just fine, but doesn't help train her in proper sleeping habits!"

"And she'll keep right on in her ways as long as she can," Olive said.

"But otherwise, the children are doing well. You know . . . they adapt." He took a drag off his cigarette and a sip of tea and continued, "They've really become quite British, picking up all sorts of things from their school and the Guest House. It's comical, really. One day Polly cut her knee at school and told us it had bled 'just shillings of blood!'"

"Oh how dear!" Olive said.

"Yes, and Patty imitates the British manner of handling a knife and fork. They call their sweaters 'woolies' and their boots 'gummies.' They seem to have lots of playmates among the other refugees. Polly kind of mothers the others and has that independent little spirit."

"Goes with her red hair," Olive interrupted.

"Exactly. And Patty, beautiful little Patty, the peacemaker, always trying to get the kids to get along. And, Penny, well, we call her our little 'tiger girl.' You don't want to cross her! She has a smile, though, that makes your heart do flip-flops and has a way of snuggling her head on your shoulder that . . . well, it just makes my arms ache for her. And she can stand now. Holding onto the crib. Can you believe it?"

Olive smiled and shook her head.

"Polly and Patty love her to death," he continued. "I'll tell you, Olive, if affection is good for the soul then Penny should grow to be a saint – everyone in that whole Guest House is devoted to her." He paused and added, "She didn't recognize me, you know."

"Of course not, Alfred, she's just a baby! But she will next time. You wait and see. She's not quite a year old yet!"

"That's just the thing. They change so much at this age. God, it was tough to leave. I know I had tears. And I saw Henry blow his nose and wipe his eyes in the taxi."

Olive patted his arm. He rubbed his face, and let his head sink into his hands. Thick waves of hair lanked through his fingers. "I just keep wondering if I'm a cad for taking the risk of returning to Wuchang – for not just taking them all back home – back to safety in the States. Then I think of the needs here . . . " he looked up. "Did I tell you a couple of my students want to be baptized? And our plans for the new Frontier Fellowship and the Young People's Conference? And you look around the city – my God, the refugees – sick, starving, homeless . . . so much to be done."

He took a last sip of tea and turned the empty porcelain cup in his hand, its intricate scene going around and around – delicate, exotic: a still blue figure fishing from a sampan, a long bending pole, concentric ripples where the pole met the water, then mountain cliffs, a pagoda, a thin waterfall, a heron, frozen in tranquillity. Dawn in Wuchang now was greeted by the familiar and not-easily-erased sight of carts winding slowly through the city streets, picking up the old, the young, and the infirm who had died the night before from starvation.

"If there is any way our Mission can help . . . and we can," he said. "But it sometimes feels like digging away at a mountain of misery with a toothpick. And then I think, should I bring the children back to this? What if there's a panic, looting, a battle? I don't know, Olive, I feel like a man divided."

"Alfred, you are doing the right thing by staying here," Olive said firmly. "The University, our middle schools, meet such great educational needs. You know as well as I do they depend on Mission support. And your students – they adore you. Why almost all the Theologs want to major in your area!"

"I know," he said. "It's just that all the sparkle of life has disappeared. I mean, I have good times, certainly, but always followed by regret and an empty feeling because Anne's not here to share memories with afterward."

"Have you heard from Dr. Wei how impressed the entire student body is that we're still here?" Olive asked in a high voice. "Such a grand demonstration of our loyalty to *them*, not a government or an army! And the needs . . . as you said, so many without a spiritual life, the poor, the terrible conditions – everywhere you look."

Her gaze penetrated his misery. He looked up at her, expectant. She turned to the window, then added softly, "Alfred, Anne wants to be here, by your side. We must keep our faith – the kind you spoke of in chapel tonight."

They were quiet then. "Thanks, Olive," he said at length. "I get so heartsick sometimes, I lose perspective. Things get all out of whack. But I know you're right." He let out a long sigh, slapped his knees, and said he'd better be going. He was exhausted from the trip back, he said. And he had a letter to write.

Sitting down once again at his typewriter, he wrote to Ma that he'd been very down in the dumps, but that a visit with Olive had cheered him. He also wrote about the trip back from Hong Kong. It had been an exhausting journey. And surprisingly dicey. A harbinger of things to come, no doubt, he wrote. There were armed guards on the train. At one point, in the middle of nowhere, the train pulled ominously to a stop. The guards rushed to the windows with their rifles. Everyone dove to the floor, not knowing if it was troops or bandits. But slowly the train pulled forward, and they continued on without a shot fired, leaving the passengers rattled and tense.

In Canton, where they had to change trains, Henry sat on the baggage while Dad went to pick up the tickets, only to discover that there was no train until 8:00 that night. The long delay turned out to be a bit of good fortune because they needed the extra time to manage the cost of the tickets. The agent had nearly bowled Dad over with the price, calmly replying to his inquiry that each ticket would cost "3,197,000 G.Y." (Gin Yuan, the Nationalist paper currency). Dad had been prepared to pay a small bribe, but this was outrageous! The station master showed him the printed schedule, and sure enough, the price was listed as the man said, no bribe involved – such was the level of inflation. Dad and Henry between them had about 68,000 G.Y. and two U.S. twenties that Dad had stuffed in his socks. The U.S.-G.Y. exchange rate was around 15,000 G.Y. to $1.00 U.S. They prayed they had enough in Hong Kong currency to make up the rest. But how to find a means of exchanging it?

Rifling through his things for hidden stashes of money, Dad came across the card of a Mr. Wu that a Mr. Giles in Hong Kong had given him in case they ran into trouble in Canton. They used the ticket agent's phone, and in a short time Mr. Wu roared up to the station in an old U.S. army jeep, his short muscular arm raised in hearty greeting. He bounded out, a stocky man with cropped hair. He tossed their bags into the jeep as if they were so much flotsam, then turned to exchange greetings and discuss the plan. Dad and Henry had some trouble deciphering exactly what he was saying. "Ve vill got to the Central Bank!" (Later they discovered he'd learned English from an old Swedish doctor.) Dad and Henry squeezed in among the bags, and they charged off, dodging pedestrians and traffic, clouds of exhaust mushrooming behind them.

Six banks later, their hearts were sunk. Not one had enough G.Y. on hand to accommodate the exchange. Over lunch a smile brightened Mr. Wu's broad face. It occurred to him that he himself might be able to exchange their money on the black market. He would need their cash, of course, and a couple of hours to round up his friends and relatives, he said. Dad and Henry looked at each other. It was risky, but they had nothing to gain by not trusting him. He left them with their bags at the restaurant where they watched the clock and tried to play cards. As the afternoon wore on, time began to crawl. Was the waiter smirking as he brought their dinner and yet another pot of tea? Was the proprietor's offer of brandy a friendly gesture or a consolation prize to two foolhardy, naive Americans?

Finally, at around 6:30 they heard the jeep honking outside, and they both leaped up to see out the window, nearly knocking over the table. Mr. Wu strode into the dark restaurant, and beaming broadly, plunked down a big stack of cash about two feet square. A short time later they were careening to the station – Mr. Wu waving and yelling and making good use of his horn. "Zay are in my vay!!" he kept saying to Dad and Henry about all those blocking their progress. At the station, he leaped out before Dad and Henry could extricate themselves and unloaded their bags in a whirl of frenetic activity. He waved off their multiple thanks, but accepted the carton of Three Castles cigarettes and a bottle of apricot brandy they had rummaged out of their bags. He roared off once again, leaving Dad and Henry blinking in disbelief at the marvel of their good fortune.

Dad sat on the luggage this time, and Henry proudly produced the money stack at the ticket counter. The agent, however, regretfully informed him that he had no record of their reservations and had sold his last ticket. Dad and Henry worked a little persuasion with what was nearly the last of their cash, and the agent, who apparently kept an extra compartment for making a little graft, was happy to oblige.

The Nationalists had removed most of the good rolling stock for the army, so their railroad car was in pretty bad shape, old and broken down. They shared their small compartment with two others, separated by a wall of luggage down the center that rose nearly up to their chins. No one was so foolish as to trust his bags to the baggage car. A porter brought them an oil lamp and informed them the train would be off sometime around 10:00 p.m.

They met their fellow travelers in the lamp light over the luggage wall – among them a man named Wang who was a member of Academia Sinica, the most learned society in China, and who spoke no English. Another passenger was one Brother Beraphim, an American lay brother of the Franciscan Fathers who spoke no Chinese. Dad and Henry spent much of the rest of the trip sharpening their translation skills. Brother Beraphim was a rough sort of fellow from New

Jersey who had worked in the labor movement and had some-how taken a job as a procurer for the Franciscans. He had a hearty contempt for "college graduate types," but was very entertaining. His job took him all over China. He knew a few foreign correspondents and had news of the war.

As they all knew, Chiang Kai-shek had stepped down in late January following the fall of Peking and Tientsin. His vice-president, Li Tsung Jen, a former general in the Kuomintang army, had taken over, tried to negotiate a peace settlement, and had been refused. Brother Beraphim con-firmed accounts that the Red Army was poised to attack Nanking, the Nationalist capital, and other cities along the Yangtze. He said he'd just been with some people from Peking who told him that, despite early reports of religious freedom and respect for foreign institutions, the reality of the situation was quite different. Apparently, foreigners had to wear arm bands identifying their nationality, their houses were searched, they were constantly interviewed, and their movements were restricted. They hadn't been thrown out, though, he added with a twinkle.

Dad and Henry asked about the fate of universities in the North. Brother Beraphim stroked the coarse growth on his chin, and said he'd learned that university courses were sub-ject to review for "anti-Communist" material, a standard that seemed to shift daily. "You college boys may be in trouble," he said, then added, "It's hard to say how it will all come down. The Reds are running things through the army up there until the political wing takes over. They don't have much of a structure – decrees come out daily and are coun-termanded daily by other decrees. It's almost as bad as the

Nationalists, except there's more enthusiasm for the cause, which isn't saying much. The Nationalists are finished. I'm pretty sure of that. Oh, they'll fight tooth and nail for cities like Nanking and Shanghai, but I doubt there'll be much of a battle in your area. Can't spread themselves too thin, plus a lot of the warlords aren't willing to commit the armies under their control – that includes your Pai Chung Hsi up in Hankow and Wuchang. I'd bet the Franciscans' last barrel of rice on that one."

The passengers in the car, chugging away to Hankow, considered his information and agreed with each other that the Communists would likely strike sometime in April before the waters of the Yangtze grew too high in summer floods.

The only battles Dad saw in Wuchang during the month of March were domestic in nature. He fought a bout of worms, thinking it was the result of the meal he'd had in Canton, but Ma wrote that Polly and Patty had them as well. In addition, he and Er Lao spent several weeks engaged in a campaign against a troop of rats who were heard massing their forces in the attic by day and attacking precious kitchen supplies and soap bars by night. Rat poison sent all but one – "Brother Rat," they called him – into retreat. Various traps and devices were arranged by Dad and Er Lao, but Brother Rat continued to outwit them until Er Lao contrived an elaborate plan involving a tin lid over the hole in the bathroom floor, the lid supported at an angle by a match stick tied by string to some bread. As he ate the bread, the lid fell over the hole, shutting off his escape route. The next morning Brother Rat was cornered in the bathroom. Er Lao, elated, enlisted the wiry and predatory cat, Nonnie, about the same size as the rat, for the final battle. My father protested, having gained too much respect and compassion for Brother Rat to bear his demise. Er Lao, aghast at such frivolous nonsense, reminded Dad of how precious their stores were.

And how right he was. By April, Wuchang was in a siege mentality. Everyone was storing up whatever was on the market. Er Lao came home with twenty-eight pounds of tinned bacon one day, and twelve pounds of canned lard the next. Butter was nowhere to be found. Powdered milk had gone off the market. The Nationalists had cut off all but military traffic on the Yangtze River from Wuchang to the coast. To the North, the Communists had shut down rice shipments coming down the Han River. In a faculty meeting, Dr. Wei urged everyone to have food reserves for at least two months, to have extra kerosene in case the power failed, and said that arrangements had been made to drill some wells for drinking water in case the water system shut down.

Inflation was escalating at even greater rates than before. An egg that cost two hundred G.Y. in the morning sold for five hundred in the afternoon. Each morning, on the way to market, Er Lao's basket was as heavy with paper currency as it was with supplies on the way back. By the end of the month, it was nearly impossible to fit enough stamps on a letter to cover the cost of sending one. At the end of February, a public notice in Hankow had announced that business could be conducted in silver, and in late March, Wuchang followed suit. Everyone on the Mission compound had begun to buy silver whenever the exchange rate was good in preparation for the total collapse of the G.Y.

Not all my father's silver went for necessities. He put

aside enough for a small nest egg for Er Lao, and in mid-March he wrote to Ma:

This morning I saw the flower man and thought of your love for flowers and could also almost hear you bargaining for some. It made me so sentimental that I parted with two of my precious silver dollars in order to buy two bushes of honeysuckle and one of roses so that they might be here for you when you return. . . . I can't put into words how much I am looking forward to having you home again. Aye Ya! It makes my heart thump against my ribs to think of it. . . .

By April, despite the conditions, my parents began to think that it was better to face the future together than apart. The Guest House in Hong Kong was filling up with refugees, some forced to find places to sleep in the lobby or hallways. They brought with them frightening tales of what they had survived, which had an obvious effect on the girls. Ma wrote that at bedtime one night she'd heard Polly and Patty end their prayers with, ". . . Please keep Daddy from being killed." She, too, began to worry for Dad's safety. He wrote back that she should assure them he was only in danger of dying from loneliness, but for the first time, the idea of moving back to the States entered their correspondence. He wrote:

Somehow I feel that if we can only get together as a family again, the future will take care of itself. If it is to be that we stay, somehow or other we can take whatever comes, and if it is that we have to go home, then it will be the same us. . . . I know the power of your will and I know that you can make the best of anything, but if you have really had enough (for which I wouldn't blame you in the least), then it might be best for us not to push that willpower to its limit. . . . Let me state my feelings as clearly as I can. I would not mind going home for your sake or for the sake of the children. There would be security and some kind of work to do, good schools and healthy, clean, fresh air for the girls. On the other hand, I honestly hope that we can see it through somehow. It isn't a family man's life, but we are here and there isn't anyone else to do the job. . . . The years here have been the happiest of my life thus far, which probably explains, in part, my reluctance to leave. The troubles seem minor in comparison to what I have found here. . . . There may be difficulties ahead, and we will need all our spiritual reserves to carry on. Therefore, you must not let your impulse to sacrifice yourself to my wishes dictate your feelings in the matter.

The minute she received his letter, she mustered her resolve. They would not be heading back to the States. She intended to let him know that "home" was now Wuchang, and that she wanted nothing more than to meet whatever lay ahead, hand in hand. She took the girls, just home from school, piled me in the big navy blue pram and set out briskly for the telegraph office, full of high purpose and energy. She was in such elevated spirits at the prospect of their all being together again, that she almost forgot to remind the girls about their walking rules. But, as they had been taught, both girls were already holding tight to her skirt, one on each side, as she pushed the carriage along.

It was a long walk to the telegraph office, down flights of shallow stone steps connecting to the streets below, along the crowded avenues. It was already quite warm in Hong Kong, and she wished she had worn a broad-brimmed hat. Along the way, she stopped in a shop for more of the blue yarn she was using to knit sweaters for the children at the orphanage in

Wuchang. She could knit with her eyes closed and turn out a sweater or baby blanket in half the time it took most of the women she knew, so she felt it was a useful way to pass the time at the Guest House. The shopkeeper, who knew her well by now, had a slice of candied fruit for each girl as they left.

She was in a hurry now to get to the telegraph office before it closed, so they passed quickly by a favorite display of carved ivory and jade. She paused briefly to consider the pomegranates at a fruit stand that was next to another of their favorites – the hat shop with its profusion of colored straws and soft, pastel felts, decked out with long feathers, fluffs of tulle, and ribbons. Moving briskly along, she glanced at her watch to check the time when her eye caught an empty space beside her skirt where Polly had been.

Heart-thumping terror. The quick, dizzying search of the nearby crowd, the tears flooding Patty's eyes at her mother's look of panic, at her darting and turning around, dragging the pram this way and that. Her frantic questions to Patty, "Where's Polly? What's happened to Polly?" Patty didn't know, she didn't know.

Suddenly, everyone around them moving in slow motion. Ma, unable to speak, afraid to let them know there was a little girl in a peach-colored school uniform. A little girl with long auburn braids and two white bows. A seven-year-old lost in a city teaming with refugees, beggars, swindlers, bandits. A little girl who could be snatched up by anyone for God-knew-what purpose. No, she must not think of that. She must go back, retrace her steps.

She grabbed me out of the pram, spools of blue yarn tumbling out, bouncing softly onto the pavement. She yanked Patty's hand and began running, but she could not catch her breath. She leaned against a wall, not a block away, suddenly unable to breathe at all. She could not move, could not make her legs go forward. Then, a great silence. People clustering around, talking to her, talking at her, moving their lips, but making no sound. She turned, pressed flat against the wall facing them, and felt she was sinking. A policeman came up, parting the crowd, lips to a whistle that she could not hear. He touched her arm, stared into her stricken face, moved his mouth. Frustrated, he knelt down next to Patty and tried to get her to stop sobbing. Finally, a faint buzzing sound, a snatch of a word, and then full-volume sound rushing in like a freight train. Her own power of speech returned, and she explained the horror of the situation to the policeman in a desperate whisper.

He sent a man to retrace her steps, but Polly was not at the hat shop, had not been back to the knitting shop. At the police station, my mother, who had not yet cried, felt faint as she filled out the report. Dr. Harth at the Guest House was called, and a car was sent to take us back there. Dr. Harth was as worried as Ma and had a hard time finding words to buck up her spirits. The police were helpful, he said. They'd leave no stone unturned. They would find her – if only he believed it himself.

We three sat with Dr. Harth in a tense knot in the lobby of the Guest House, Ma's face devoid of expression, a running prayer repeating itself over and over in her head. "Dear God, bring her back. Dear God, bring her back." Women wrung their hands and offered cool cloths. The American Consulate was contacted. A group of men at the Guest House had formed a search party. They were just preparing to leave when John Mason happened to look out. A little girl in a peach-colored uniform was rounding the corner into the drive and approaching the steps up to the Guest House. The dark red hair, the two white bows. "Mrs. . . . Mrs. Starratt," he said in a faltering voice, unable to take his eyes off the child. Then, turning his head, he cried, "Anne, Anne! Come quick!" Ma and the others charged to the wide-open entrance. Everyone froze in place as Polly, panting slightly, climbed each step with steady resolve. Ma held her hand to her mouth, whispered, "Oh, my glory!" then rushed down the steps to gather Polly into her arms.

Polly hugged Ma tightly, relieved that Ma wasn't lost after all. But the adult commotion bubbling and swelling around her confused her utterly. Why were the grown-ups crying and shouting? "Something terrible, something terrible has happened," she thought, and she began to cry. When the noise settled down, when she was firmly ensconced on Ma's lap, the tearful Patty by her side, the adults explained to her why they were so upset. She told them that she thought that she and Ma and Patty and Penny were looking at the hat shop just like they always did, but then her mother wasn't there. She looked and looked. There were too many people. Her mother was lost! And so she did the only thing she could think of. She came back home. Didn't they know she knew the way? She'd been along those streets dozens of times, she said.

The fragility of life was never so close to Ma's heart as it was that night. She sat up in bed, thinking of their little white house in Lincoln, Massachusetts, wondering what they were doing in this strange, dangerous, unpredictable place. Moonlight stretched across the girls' cots, their rumpled bed covers moving slightly with each breath. Precious Jasmine, Precious Beauty, Precious Love. Her precious three. How good they had been, adjusting to the new school, to the new set of children, dressing themselves, tamping their shoes upside down each morning to check for scorpions and centipedes, as if it were the most natural thing in the world to do. She wanted to gather them up in her arms. She wanted to hold them forever, to be held herself, to feel the very weight of her husband's frame leaning in toward hers, their arms around each other, and somehow, the three girls nestled between them. The little frame house in New England, that's where she wanted to picture the scene, but the image would not hold. There could be no little frame house, no rectory, no New England, without Alfred. And so, the white frame house kept dissolving into images of their house in Wuchang.

But summer was coming, and there were severe warnings against keeping small children in the steaming heat and unbearable humidity of a Wuchang summer. It posed particular danger to Western children who had less resistance to disease than Chinese children. They were struck with prickly heat that would quickly turn into boils all over their bodies, leaving them too depleted to fight diseases like dysentery and tuberculosis. The latter was rampant among the Chinese. The former could be equally deadly. One after another, the headstones in the foreign cemetery marked the graves of missionary children under five years of age. Even adults succumbed. Arthur Rollins told Dad one evening about an attack of dysentery he'd had several summers before, explaining that within six hours of the first cramp he was too weak to go out for help and was luckily rescued by a neighbor. He said his grown son, Peter, had had a case a while back, and within a week, every bone in his body was visible through his skin, despite the fact that he'd been a good deal overweight the week before. A child would not have survived. Everyone, including Dr. Wei and the Church Mission House in New York, agreed that Wuchang was no place for children in the summer months. Kuling was the answer.

Ma knew that as she contemplated the future. Like many others from the Mission, my parents took refuge from the heat during the summer months in the mountains of Kuling, about a hundred miles down the Yangtze from Wuchang. There they had bought a small cottage with cool stone verandahs. She knew that it was fruitless to consider returning to Wuchang in the summer months unless they could get to Kuling.

Kuling – isolated, remote, of no strategic importance, high up in the mountains away from crowds and refugees and war. Kuling, where the sunsets streaked across the sky in hues so brilliant it made hearts ache. The mountain peaks, green up close, fading to blue and gray in the distance. Their own little garden of carrots, corn, spinach and cucumber. The long draughts of cool mountain air. The fields of black-eyed Susans. The well-worn paths winding through the grasses to ancient temple ruins. The family picnics on the rocks where my father taught my sisters to swim in deep, clear pools beneath streaming horsetail falls. Kuling – lyrical, lush, safe.

The problem was getting there. By April, the journey by train to Kiukiang, a nearby entry to the mountains of Kuling, was next to impossible because of poor connections, maladministration, and occasional riots along the line. Of the small boats still allowed to run on the river, the Wushieh launch was possible for the two-day trip, but it was alive with bedbugs, according to those who had recently been on it. In any case, it had temporarily stopped running. Soldiers had fired on it, and the owners were afraid of piracy. There were a few Chinese junks, larger sailing vessels, heading that way, but that meant being stacked in without private quarters in extremely unsanitary conditions, increasing the risk of disease. So, until transportation opened up again, Kuling was out of the question. And if Kuling was out of the question, then so was Wuchang. The central Church Mission House in New York considered it too costly to transport the families and their belongings to Wuchang, only to have them return again to Hong Kong because they were unable to reach Kuling for the summer months. There was the added risk of losing their room at the Guest House. Thus, it became clear that a spring return to Wuchang was not to be.

It seemed that if Wuchang would surrender to the Communists, then life could start up again, and there would be an end to the uncertainty of the situation. If it happened in the spring, the launches might be running by June, and they could get to Kuling. Or, if it seemed impossible to carry on, they could plan to return to the States. If only the Communists would launch their offensive soon, they thought. The sooner, the better.

The Communists obliged. On April 21 the Red Army crossed the Yangtze in a massive assault that covered four hundred miles between Anking to the south and Nanking to the north. In short order, Li Tsung Jen and the Nationalist government fled south to Canton.

Five

HE FALL OF Nanking left little doubt that the Nationalists were on the run. One way or another Wuchang would soon be in Communist hands. On May 3, the Armed Forces radio station in Manila announced that there was no future for American enterprise in China, and warned missionaries not to stick by their posts in the belief that they would be able to carry on. There were no plans to evacuate Americans out of the Wuhan area, however. The job of evacuation had been conducted the previous November, an assistant to the Consulate reminded them the next day. Those who hadn't left in November had been told it was their last chance. Besides, there were riots along the rail lines, steamships had stopped running, and the airport had been closed for months due to crumbling runways.

The Mission was largely unfazed. They had made their choice. Yet, a feeling of the end of things began to creep in.

Posted notices of scheduled events were followed by the initials D.V. which stood for *Deus volens* (God willing). "PLANNING COMMITTEE FOR ST. HILDA'S SUMMER CONFERENCE MAY 23, D.V.," a notice might say. Over afternoon tea, at chance meetings on campus, at evening sing-alongs, rumors circulated about conditions under the Communists: "Did you hear that churches in northern cities are empty – people are that afraid of religious intimidation!" "Why, I've heard that theological courses are banned!" "That's nothing, the news from Cheeloo University is that foreigners are forbidden from teaching altogether!"

Dr. Wei told Dad and Henry he was sure that once the Communists arrived it would be much easier to bring the families back, and work could continue under the new order. His enthusiasm overwhelmed darker opinions about life under the new order. In fact, it was difficult to get a word in edgewise. He talked about a quick surrender, about what courses they'd teach in the fall, and how they'd teach in private homes if it came to that. It was hard to counter such spirit, especially from such a respected leader.

No one knew exactly how to prepare for the change in power. The Nationalists had thrown up a blockade, so buying things on the market was increasingly difficult. On their end of the compound, Dad, the Camps, and Olive began to live off their stores. Hopefully, they'd be leaving for Kuling by the end of June. If not, Dad had every intention of getting to Hong Kong to wait out the summer with Ma until, together, they could determine if returning to Wuchang would make sense.

In April, the Mission House in New York had sent three months advance pay in case the postal service failed. By May

the silver dollar was worth seven million G.Y., and banks did-
n't have nearly enough currency to cash checks from the U.S.
If they could not use their U.S. paychecks in the summer, and
their stores of silver were depleted, it would shut the Mission
down.

A more immediate fear was the anarchy that would doubt-
less follow the departure of the Nationalists. As the faint sound
of distant cannon grew louder, students and professors organized nightly campus patrols. Dad and Papa Camp were
assigned to St. Hilda's School. In town, the merchants and
police bargained over the cost of a bribe to ensure the police
would stay and keep order when the army left. The police
demanded, and finally got, great quantities of silver. When he
was renewing his residence permit at the police station, Dad
asked if the police would indeed stay on. "Probably not," the
permit official shrugged. "We have accepted their bribe, but
we must also consider ourselves. Our best protection against
the Red Army is to be somewhere else."

Peter Rollins had a letter from his brother in Nanking telling
about the panic there. Apparently, after a day of widespread
looting, the citizens organized a voluntary defense corps to
patrol the streets. From that point on, he said, the looting was
orderly, more democratic. The defense corps made people stand
in line at smashed window fronts, overseeing the looting so that
more people could get a share of the stolen goods!

Dad and Er Lao decided they should hide valuables in the
attic and a good supply of silver currency in a hole in the linen
closet wall. They boarded up the hole and smoothed it over.
Then Dad closed the closet door and snapped the big Yale lock
shut with a flourish, after which he and Er Lao stared at the
door for a while, willing it to open. Unfortunately, Er Lao's key

ring, including the key for the Yale lock, was on a shelf on the other side of the now-locked door.

Er Lao, who had clearly missed his calling as an engineer, fetched a brick, a ladder, a sieve, a broom, and some string. Dad steadied the wobbly ladder as Er Lao climbed up and broke the glass transom over the door frame with the brick. Then, with some effort, he slid his long torso halfway into the transom. With exacting dexterity, he swept the heavy key ring from the closet shelf into the dangling sieve, and they were, as Er Lao said, "back in business."

The business of the Mission and the University continued during those first weeks of May. Classes were taught, services held, patients at the hospital and clinics seen and treated. The lights flashed on and off three times each evening at 11:30. No one knew why – and no one bothered to find out. Dad worked on the last chapter of his thesis, a lecture series for the St. Hilda's Conference, an article for the *Theological Review*, and spent numerous hours with Loh Chung Ku on his final term paper.

Temperatures soared into the nineties, and everyone was dripping. Dad's collar wilted like a damp rag under his cassock as the bishop baptized Li Shan To on May 10. At the evening chapel service, his good friend Frank Boulton preached, calling for a creative fellowship in the church to meet the exigencies of the times.

Despite, or perhaps because of, the "exigencies of the times," a new spirit was afoot in the Mission. Several like-minded souls, my father one of the leaders among them, formed a new fellowship group. They called it the Frontier Fellowship. It was intended as a means of joining students of all the Christian faiths represented at the University – Baptist,

Presbyterian, Anglican (Episcopalian), Wesleyan, and others
– into an all-inclusive, interfaith union. At the time, the very
concept of "interfaith" was considered radical.

Dad and the others hoped to foster the belief that the
bonds of common faith were more important than minor
denominational differences and the belief that that union
would lead them all toward better solutions for the problems
that beset Wuchang. They addressed ways to band together
in projects of service to those in need. They also addressed
students' concerns about the intersection of faith with the
coming change in government. Over one hundred students
participated, breaking into several groups and eagerly dis-
cussing such questions as, "If both Christians and Communists
believe in change toward social justice, what are the differences?" and "Can social change be accomplished without vio-
lence?" The professors asked the questions, then sat back and
let the students carry the discussion. In the second week, they
were asked, "What difference does it make to believe in God?"
and "Does a belief in God make Christians morally superior to
Communists?" To this last, the students responded with a
resounding *No!* It was uplifting to hear their lively discussion
about the essential goodness of all men, regardless of religious
belief, and the power of faith to extend man to something other
than himself.

In a letter to Ma following the Fellowship meeting in the
second week of May, Dad wrote:

*. . . If it is anything like we want it to be, it [the Frontier Fellowship]
will be a vehicle to give expression to the longings of these young
people. . . . I think it is the beginning of a movement that will bring new
life to the University in terms of Christian action. I came away thank-*

*ful that I have been here to be a part of this, and hoping that I can con-
tinue on here at Huachung. . . . This is religion as it really lives in me –
friendship finding expression in common concern for very real and practical things, and the whole gathered up in common loyalty to a conception
of the loving will of God. This is more than rites, more than pious wishes . . . it is alive and it has power. . . . May God grant me the ability to
carry it to wherever I go.*

His close association with founding members, especially
Tim Yagear, contributed as well to his personal growth. He
continued the letter with this thought, *"I hope that as I grow
older my practice continues to grow more and more in harmony with
the basic things I believe in – and I think that the end of that process
would be a life like Tim's, for I think his whole way of life is simply a
translation of his faith into action."* He finished the letter as he
always did, wishing she could be there to share it all with
him, saying, *"Without my precious 4, I seem to live 1/5 of a life."*

A few days later, he was searching in his bedroom for a
book, when Er Lao came racing up the stairs, out of breath,
shouting, "The Communists! They're here – marching into
Hankow this very minute!" Dad blinked up at him in disbelief. On this perfectly peaceful, hot afternoon in May, without
so much as a cannon fired?

"The Communists? How? Who told you?" he asked Er Lao.
He glanced quickly at the wall calendar – it was May 15.

"Miss Tomlin's cook, Loh Shih Fu. He just came back
from Hankow. He said –"

Er Lao was interrupted by noise and commotion downstairs – doors banging and voices calling, "Alfred! Alfred!
Have you heard?"

Dad rushed to the stairs and leaned over the banister toward the flushed faces of Morgan Reilly, Philip Stowe, and Olive Tomlin looking up at him. Rushing down to them, he kept saying, "I can't believe it!"

Dr. Reilly quickly explained that Dr. Guilford at the Union Hospital across the river had called to say that the police and the army had left the city at one end, and the Red Army was marching in at the other.

Everyone moved into the kitchen, talking over each other in disjointed fragments, not knowing whether to be relieved or scared. Suddenly, the entire house shook under a massive explosion somewhere nearby. Olive and Philip fell to their knees, arms over their heads. An upstairs window shattered, dishes clattered to the floor, and chairs skittled sideways as if animated to seek protection. When it was over, Dad, Er Lao and Dr. Reilly rushed to the windows, but could see nothing. Lesser explosions continued intermittently for a time. The Camps came over and told them that the Nationalist troops were blowing up transportation installments in Hankow as they departed – the airport, a bridge, and the steel barges along the waterfront of Hankow that were used as landing places for the river steamers.

At 6:30 a message came from St. Hilda's asking for protection, so Dad and Mr. Camp packed a few overnight things and got on their bicycles. Aside from a few soldiers running toward the railway station, the streets were eerily quiet. As they reached the big East Gate, they heard the sounds of pandemonium and then saw one of the last trains slowly pulling out from the station. They biked over to join a small crowd at some distance from the tracks, then stood astride their bicycles watching the awful spectacle. The sight brought to mind a beehive. Hardly a square inch of the big engine and the cars behind it was visible beneath the swarming bodies. Most of them were soldiers, but there were many civilians as well, clutching and grabbing at others who seemed to be hanging on by their teeth. They could hear the mob yelling and fighting, could see them hauling people off in an attempt to get a spot for themselves. Wisely, the engineer kept the train moving on to avoid further riot, and a great many fell into the ditch as the train gained momentum.

When they arrived at St. Hilda's, they found things were peaceful. The headmistress of the school was grateful for their presence. Secretly, Dad wondered what they could do in the face of a mob, but was glad to be of service. She told him in Chinese that the "rabble" would not dare harm two foreign men. Dad had his doubts. They spent the early evening watching fires burning across the river in Hankow, flames licking toward the sky, sprays of embers shooting up like fireworks. Explosions continued, and the night passed with the sounds of whistles, gongs, much shouting, and the "pop-pop" rattle of Japanese rifles coming from the direction of the University compound. But there was no sign of troops.

Dad found a book next to his cot called *The Strumpet Wind* and read it cover to cover by the flickering light of a fat, wax-dripping candle. The next morning he couldn't remember a thing he'd read. He and Papa Camp biked home at dawn past some abandoned military barracks that were already stripped bare for firewood by the local populace.

At home, Mama Camp told them about the night on the Huachung compound. At around 1:00 in the morning a gang of deserters from the Kuomintang army was marauding outside the compound wall, trying to get in. Safety volunteers from the city were passing by and told the patrols to alert the Mission to turn on all their lights and come out of their houses to the gate. Then the safety volunteers shot off their rifles and created a whistle-and-gong racket at one end of the compound. The missionaries at the other end shouted to the soldiers that the noise was the Red Army coming their way. The soldiers fell for the ruse and fled.

"So that's what all that noise was!" Dad said.

A bit later, he and Er Lao walked over to a nearby hill to watch the last train winding away in the valley below. It stopped for a time near a bridge over a gorge and then moved on. Five minutes later there was a thundering shudder that shook the ground and rattled their teeth. When it was over they stood up to see huge chunks of the distant stone bridge tumbling into the tributary below in a rising cloud of smoke and debris.

"So, the railroad's finished – I guess they'll blow out every bridge between here and Changsha," Dad said.

"Just so," Er Lao nodded. "But you will find a way out."

As they ate supper, a messenger from Bishop Tsang in Hankow brought word to the compound that Communist troops had indeed marched into Hankow in orderly columns, carrying great banners with pictures of Mao Tse-tung before them, and that they planned to be in Wuchang the following day. He also brought a handbill the soldiers had passed out telling foreigners to stay where they were, but not to expect to get away with being hypocrites by pretending to be in favor of the new order.

On the morning of May 17, the tinny sound of a small marching band drew Dad and Philip to the Ku Chia P'o Gate. There they saw the young Boon School boys marching off to greet the arriving Red Army. The University students followed en masse to the center of town. As ordered, the foreign community stayed on the compound. Little did any of them realize, standing on the familiar grounds of the campus that May morning, that they were witnessing not just another military takeover, but a vast revolution, a People's Revolution that would alter China forever and have a profound effect on world order.

The students returned to campus sometime later in high spirits, waving hundreds of little red paper flags that said, "Welcome People's Liberation Army!" Many of them carried great banners of Mao's impassive face, and others of Chiang Kai-shek being tortured. Two of Dad's students, a boy and a girl, came brightly over to Dad and Philip, each holding a pole that supported a banner. Cheerfully they described all they had seen. How many soldiers there were! How friendly and polite they were! They chatted away, eager and excited to share their experience, the banner fluttering between them. It depicted the execution of Uncle Sam and John Bull, accompanied by the slogan, "Down with American and British Imperialism!"

Within the week, the students requested several days off from classes to carry out a program of lectures to the local peasants and to study Mao's book, *The New Democracy,* as they had been told to do by the army generals. The faculty met, and after much deliberation, they voted to grant their request. They agreed that the students were too excited to focus on their work anyway. Dr. Wei then informed those present that when the political wing of the government arrived, there would be a variety of restrictions. Foreigners would likely be confined to the compound. Interviews would be conducted with attempts to incite anger. Imprisonment would result if one rose to the bait. He also said that that very morning he had pulled down a poster on the chapel door that said, "Religion Is a Tool of Foreign Imperialists." So, he concluded, things might be difficult for a time, but it would all sort itself out. Everyone gave a vote of confidence to Dr. Wei for carrying them through the previous months with morale intact. Everyone was committed to seeing the semester through.

Everyone, it seemed, except the students. They spent most of their time practicing dances and singing folk songs. The clanging gongs in the gymnasium nearly drove everyone mad. It was said that several zealous students went so far as to capture a few of their less enthusiastic fellow students and lock them in a room. They proudly reported their capture to the Communist authorities, who promptly told them to go back and unlock the prisoners. "We will thank you to go back to your classes and leave any such work to us!" said the authorities.

The students formed a union and sent around a petition to abolish comprehensive exams. Exams, they said, were a feudalistic practice. They were undemocratic! Students plastered the administration building with slogans: "More Time for Study – Down with Exams!" "We Are Against Harmful Traditions!" The words were in English, presumably aimed at the "reactionary and imperialist" foreign faculty. The faculty, Chinese and foreign, voted unanimously to maintain the exams, and the seniors went on strike on May 31. Dad was crushed to learn that some of his prized theological students were among the strike organizers.

Not three days later, the students appeared with mops

and water, took down every one of their posters, and returned to classes. Then they sent a letter to each faculty member saying that they wanted to clear the air by inviting them to a tea given by the senior class in Stokes Hall the following afternoon. Somewhat confused, the faculty complied. At the party Dr. Wei said he was a little ashamed of the students, but could forgive and forget, and they all joined in singing "Blessed Be the Tie That Binds."

Dad and Henry walked back to the house together after the tea, shaking their heads over the naiveté of the students, and glad that things were back to normal, or what passed for normal.

The very next day, June 4, a large public meeting was organized in town to air student grievances. Representatives from the various schools were elected to describe the conditions at their schools. The Boon School, St. Hilda's, and Huachung University received the lowest marks. The students accused Huachung of being a stronghold of reactionary imperialism where the purpose of education was subordinate to the attempt to make the students Christians. They said Dr. Wei was an autocrat who never consulted students and workmen on the compound before making decisions – that there were too many rules and too many examinations. Such was the plight of students at this unreformed, undemocratic institution!

The faculty was stunned, but at the same time they understood something of the forces pulling at these young people. The great majority continued to be on friendly terms with their professors, and when they weren't gathered in self-criticism groups or practicing folk dances, they continued to attend class. But they were clearly taken with their newfound power – like students everywhere, they relished rebellion.

True, they sometimes appeared to have little understanding that it would take more than songs and dances and a "cooperative attitude" to fix the problems at hand. They were young, idealistic, naive and easily manipulated. But it was also understood that, despite their privileged status as students, a privilege accorded so few in China, they were aware of the vast landscape around them – the tens of thousands starving to death, the generations of grinding poverty, and the years of government corruption that left in its wake a crumbling infrastructure that could not begin to address public health, housing, sanitation, and inflation. They were sensitive to the less fortunate, perhaps because they were attending a religious institution.

And so it was with a mixture of understanding and heartbreaking disappointment that the faculty reacted to outbursts of extreme propaganda from students they had nurtured. For the foreign faculty, of course, there were additional notes of sadness. It appeared extremely unlikely that they would have a place in the new regime, and many knew their time was up.

Some, especially those without children, continued to hold out hope, but Dad and Henry were ready to go as soon as they could. It was pie in the sky to imagine, as some did, that the U.S. would recognize the Communist government. Americans would soon be seen as enemies of the state, and perhaps already were. Er Lao was anxious for them to get to safety. He'd heard troubling rumors on the streets, disturbing enough that he'd refused to share them with Dad.

The problem was getting the necessary papers and permission to leave the country. Shortly after the occupation, Dr. Wei met with one of the Communist generals who was an old Huachung graduate. The general was sympathetic to their plight, but he said that at present there was no way for the army to grant travel to aliens. These were matters of foreign affairs and had to be relayed to central headquarters, which he said he would do. But nothing came of it.

Soon, those who could grant permission arrived. In bits and pieces during the month of June, the political structure of the new order began to be erected, and with it came a variety of regulations. Everyone who owned silver was told to exchange it for Communist currency. By May 26 the price of a silver dollar had jumped from 350 to 1000 in Communist currency. Communist bank notes were sure to be nearly as useless as Nationalist currency had been a few weeks before. Not surprisingly, the civilian officials were not too successful at getting people to exchange their silver for the inflated bank notes, so they decided to enlist the students in the campaign. In mid-June they instructed schools and universities to tear up examinations so the students could go out on the streets to educate people to turn over their silver to the banks at the official exchange rates, a form of education that suddenly was considered much more productive than examinations. The students complied happily.

Regulations piled on top of regulations. On June 23 a notice went up that all foreigners were to report to the police station to re-register. The notice contained other rules: Foreigners must submit to the police at all times; all firearms must be turned in; use of field glasses during air raids was not permitted; cameras were forbidden at all times.

Dad and Philip went down to the police station together. A surly soldier stopped them at the entrance gate with a stream of invectives in a dialect neither Philip nor Dad could understand. He made threatening gestures with his rifle. Finally, he brought his gun to shoulder height and took aim. Another sentry then told them in their own dialect what the soldier wanted – he wanted them off their bicycles. They complied and the bicycles were wheeled off behind the station.

Inside, they found what looked like half of Wuchang crowded into the lobby. When they made it through the lines, the registration official rustled papers on his desk, finally eyed them, and asked where they had parked their cars. "Cars? We don't own any cars!" they said. He refused to believe them. After much angry talk, he asked about the University cars. Philip told them about the truck.

"Ah Ha!" said their grand inquisitor. "Have the chauffeur bring it here at once!" Dad and Philip said not only was there no chauffeur, the truck was broken. They had to explain in some detail that a truck with a broken motor could not move. The exasperated official stood up and waved them away with a promise that the truck would be "requisitioned."

But what about our registration permits? Dad and Philip wanted to know. Registration permits? The man removed his glasses and wiped the lenses vigorously. Registration permits? He had heard of no such thing. They must come back for those another day; perhaps tomorrow there would be such permits. He put his round black glasses back on and motioned the next in line to come forward.

But Dad and Philip remained where they were. "And travel passes?" they asked tentatively.

"We have no regulations covering travel passes," the official said. "That is up to the Foreign Affairs Committee in Peking! Now move on!" A nearby guard helped them get the point that their interview was over.

They were not confined to the compound, but excursions

outside could be dangerous. Soldiers and officials gained political stature by harassing foreigners. Locals took up the practice, but it was sometimes lighthearted. "Kow pi-tse, yao pu yao tse-tze?" (Big nose, do you want a rickshaw?) a coolie called out to Dad one day in town.

"Ai pi-tse, ni you mei you tse-tze?" (Short nose, have you got a rickshaw?) Dad called back, and the crowd joined in with a good laugh.

More soldiers arrived. Many of them were Kuomintang deserters, unfriendly and angry. They took over the Boon School gymnasium, the convent chapel, and all but one of the student dormitories on the Huachung campus. They entered houses at will, ground cigarette butts into the floor, and looked about suspiciously at radios and flashlights. Their bad behavior could not be reported for fear of reprisals. Some, though, were mere boys who spent their free time on the kindergarten playground, climbing three and four at a time on the see-saw, breaking it once, apologizing, and moving on to the swings.

In the midst of an ongoing war, there was little the new government could do to improve conditions beyond trying to feed their soldiers, end the war, and win over the people to their ideals of social reform. On the porch one morning in early July, Dad was reading an account of some new reforms in the newspaper when something strange caught his eye. Something strange and white in the garden by the roots of the honeysuckle he'd planted for Ma. He put the paper down and cautiously peered at the object, which he saw was a soiled quilt. Then he saw the tiny hand reaching out toward the steps, little fingers curled upward. He called Er Lao, Philip, Olive, Mama Camp! And they came running. But none of them could do a thing to breathe life into the thin little body. Had it been alive when it had been left there? They could not tell. He did not write to Ma about how they buried the baby beneath the honeysuckle, how the image of the starved child haunted his sleep for months to come.

But he did write to Bob Curry in Lenox, Massachusetts – that very night. It was Bob who had gotten him into the ministry when he worked as a camp counselor at Camp O-AT-KA in Maine. Bob was now headmaster of the Lenox School, an Episcopal school for boys. Back in December, when Bob learned about our evacuation to Hong Kong, he had written about a couple of parish jobs in the Berkshires that Dad might be interested in. Suddenly, Dad was very interested. He knew the parish jobs were probably long gone, but he told Bob he'd even take a teaching job at Lenox, though he thought he might be "something of a greenhorn" at teaching secondary school. He would need a little coaching, perhaps, and he knew the money was not great, but he said that about now money was the least important thing to him as long as he had enough to keep the family going. He ended by saying that he had little hope of their being able to carry on in Wuchang, that he'd lost the cottage in Kuling when the Communists took it over, and that it looked like they'd be home by summer if he could ever get out – "home, penniless and with little more than the clothes on our backs, but home." He attached a quick note to Ma telling her to mail the letter to Bob as soon as she received it. A student of Dad's was heading to Hong Kong and would hand-deliver the letter to Ma when he got there.

The mails had been even more erratic since the takeover. The Nationalist blockade around Communist areas made it difficult for mail to get to Hong Kong. Mail between Communist areas and the U.S. was forbidden. The telegraph office ran intermittently. After the arrival of the Red Army, he didn't hear from Ma until June 15 when he'd received the following telegram:

LETTERS STILL ARRIVING STOP LOVING MISSING
AND WANTING YOU STOP FOUR DARLINGS

Grateful that his four darlings knew he was all right, Dad stood the telegram up on his desk with what he called his "morale boosters" – a picture of his girls on a swing, our passport picture, a picture of Ma, demure in her wedding veil, and one of her laughing, so vibrant, so beautiful she almost shimmered through the glass when he looked at her.

It was now July 8, and he had not received a word since her telegram. Not knowing if his letters were getting through, he entrusted his student not only with his letter, but the carbon copies of all his letters to her since the liberation.

A day or so later he was stunned to receive a packet of three letters postmarked May 15, May 20, and May 27. He hurried home, waving them triumphantly at Er Lao and Philip in the kitchen. In his study, he arrayed the delicious cache of envelopes on his desk and sat down to nurse the prickly heat on his thigh with medicine and cool rags. Then he opened the first of the letters. Amazingly, it contained a letter from Bob Curry to Ma. Bob explained that he'd been serving as an interim preacher at St. Paul's Church in Stockbridge, Massachusetts, a town in the Berkshire Mountains, near Lenox. They were searching for a rector, and he hoped that "Al would have sense enough to get out of China" and consider the position. The church had been without a rector for some time, he said, and they were willing to hold the position and were hoping to hear of his interest in June. The letter was dated May 11.

Dad crumpled the letter in his hand and stood up. The wet rag slipped to the floor. Aye Ya! Stockbridge! He'd seen it once – a beautiful little town! A perfect little town! A parish in the Berkshires, slipping through his hands as he sat half a world away, powerless to change his situation!

And his situation seemed desperate. Shanghai had fallen to the Communists at the end of May. The Nationalists had then launched what they called an "unprecedented" air offensive against troop concentrations and all means of transportation in Communist-held China. They warned citizens to stay away from railroads, waterfronts, and highways. They began sporadic bombing of Hankow on June 15, aiming at river steamers. In Wuchang, anti-American sentiment was growing. American checks were declared illegal. Theological courses could no longer be taken for credit, and the Communists planned to take over the middle schools and Huachung to set up their own university for the summer – and very likely for all time. He had to get out.

You could not travel without a pass. And no one would issue passes, though they "might look into it soon." Dad and Henry had been told in mid-June that Chinese citizens could leave China, but foreigners could not. The next week they learned the Military Control Commission would consider the matter of foreign travel within the week. Then a week later, they were told to check with the Alien Control Board – that a policy would be developed. But the Alien Control Board claimed they had no authority and no interest in granting travel passes for foreigners just now. They had more important matters before them. Come back next week or the week after. We may have a policy then, they were told. Each time they contemplated slipping out, they'd get a signal that passes might become available. Their quest became almost laughable, surreal. They were imprisoned without the trappings of prison. They vacillated between hope of legal transport and risking everything.

Dad and Henry explored every possible route out – by sailboat six hundred miles down the Yangtze to Shanghai and from there another six or seven hundred miles down the coast to Hong Kong; by small boat to Yoyang, and thence overland through the battle lines to Canton. Any trip involving small boats or walking on foot left one easy prey for bandits. With or without a pass, they would have to make the trip penniless. Silver would be either stolen or seized in general inspections and exchanged for Communist currency. And, of course, Communist currency would be useless when they reached Nationalist territory. Dad investigated traveling with a group of smugglers who worked for respectable Hankow businessmen, but if they were caught without passes *and* in the company of smugglers, they risked being thrown in jail or being shot on the spot. As Er Lao told him many times, it was better to be a live husband in Wuchang than a dead one somewhere along the way to Hong Kong. Travel with passes was dangerous enough. Travel without them meant risking one's life in a thousand ways. Dad was just desperate enough to consider it.

That night he tossed in a fitful sleep on the damp sheets, dreaming. He was crossing the Berkshires with a baby in his arms, trying to get to Hong Kong, but he was stopped by Bob Curry in a soldier's uniform demanding a travel pass. He awoke with a start. There was a strange sound in his room. He lay still for a few minutes and heard it again – like someone banging on his screen. He turned to look at the screen, and in the dim light of pre-dawn, a dark object flew up from the floor, hit the screen again, and flopped back down. Unable to distinguish what it was, he quickly went down for the flashlight, which he could not find. Er Lao woke up, and when they returned to the room, there was nothing in front of the screen. They lit a small oil lamp and held it aloft. There, in a shadow by the bureau, the identity of their mysterious intruder was revealed. With its back feathers pressed against the wall, a young wild duck looked up at them. They stared back at it – Er Lao appraising and dismissing the dinner possibilities, Dad sensing the duck's torment. Together they cautiously approached the creature. Amid a great flapping of wings, they eventually gathered their prisoner into their arms and cradled it between them as it struggled, craning its neck. Moving as a unit, they took the stairs one at a time – the duck, Er Lao and Dad. They side-stepped out the door to the porch. At the ledge they opened their arms and lifted them up. The duck froze for a moment, and then went winging its way toward the river. They watched until it was a tiny dot against the light breaking out across the eastern sky. They watched long after it had disappeared from view.

Six

THE FANS HIGH up on the ceiling stirred the air, but didn't help to relieve the heat. It was the middle of August, and Hong Kong was steaming. Ma fanned herself with a silk and bamboo fan, dipping it down periodically to cool the faces of the girls. Polly and Patty had taken turns chasing me down in the waiting room, but now we were all too hot and flushed to move. The Chinese nurse, prim and pleasant, motioned to Ma.

"The doctor will see you now," she said, and ushered us past a row of patients on a bench and into the office. Long rays of sun slanted through the partially closed wooden slats on the tall shuttered windows, casting alternating stripes on the glass cabinets and across Dr. Wesley's desk. He pulled a set of X-ray plates from two separate envelopes. Ma sat down to wait for the results.

"I'm sorry to report that things have not improved, but at

least they're not worse," he said, holding both Polly and Patty's X-rays against a lighted screen. "You can see here, here, and over here a spot. Disappointing really, and of some concern, especially in Polly's case – our little survivor." The doctor was referring to Polly's heart condition. She had been born with a leak in her heart – what they used to call a "blue baby." When she was eighteen months old she had open-heart surgery in Boston – an experimental procedure and one of the first open-heart surgeries ever performed. She had a long scar on her chest, but was otherwise healthy. Naturally, she was watched carefully.

As Ma listened to the doctor's report, the girls leaned in heavily against her legs. She shifted me to her other knee and felt a thin line of sweat trickle down one leg. But she felt too immobilized by the news and the weight of the children to reach for the fan inside her purse.

"It's early-stage tuberculosis, of course not bad yet, but I'd hate to see them have further exposure. Like I said, I worry about the crowded conditions of the Guest House – and the extreme heat of a Hong Kong summer doesn't give them much bounce to fight it off. And now here's Penny with worms again."

"I know, I know," Ma groaned.

"Is there any way you can get them out of Hong Kong? I'd like to see you take them home, Mrs. Starratt. I really advise it. Or at least, get them to a cooler climate. Any word on your husband?"

"I haven't had any letters since July when a student brought some out. But five days ago, I think it was August 10, I got a telegram dated August 6 that said, 'Possibilities suddenly favorable. Please wait' – something like that. No word since, but I don't want to leave if he's about to get out. . . . Of course, I have no idea if he really is on his way out." She looked at the doctor and then down at the girls. "I just keep thinking he's almost here – praying he is, anyway."

"Well, I suggest you book passage on one of the President Line ships. I've heard they're taking U.S. refugees out at almost no cost."

She nodded in silent agreement.

"Could take weeks to get a reservation, of course." Dr. Wesley seemed agitated. "Any other possibilities before that? What about the island of Lan Tao? It's only a ferry ride away. Aren't there some Missions in the mountains up there?" he asked.

"Yes, as a matter of fact the Baptist Mission has a summer retreat up there. My friend Sally Stevens is going in a few days. I was going to go, but then thought Alfred might be out at any minute. But yes, I'll try to get in with her."

"Not to worry too much, Mrs. Starratt," Dr. Wesley said rising, "but especially for Polly's sake, that would be best. We have to think of her heart. The mountain air up there is just what she needs, and Patty too, and little Penny." He gave us a wink.

Back at the Guest House, Ma immediately checked her mail, then caught up with Sally Stevens and explained the situation. She had been reluctant to spend the money to go in halfway on a cottage in Lan Tao, but there was no question now. Mrs. Stevens was delighted. She had two young children of her own. She and Ma had become good friends, taking the children to Victoria Park, to the Peak for sunset picnics, and sometimes by trolley all the way to Repulse Bay for a day at the beach.

Ma found Dr. Harth in his office. He sat next to her, lit his pipe and listened thoughtfully as she reviewed the options. He agreed that she should, she must, book passage on a ship right away, but that for now Lan Tao was the answer. He promised to get word to her as soon as possible if Alfred made it out before the month was up. "Perhaps this will be best, not only for the children's sake, but for you, Anne," he said, taking her hand. "You've been under great stress, and who knows, perhaps some time away will not only relieve your spirit, but bring him back all the quicker. A watched pot never boils. . . . I'll get word to the Baptist Mission. I think you will find them wonderful people and most welcoming."

After a supper of "slippery sly" (the girls' term for rice noodles) in the dining room, followed by their favorite dessert, buttered bread and sugar, Polly and Patty settled down in the lobby with some copies of the *London Illustrated*. They loved the pictures of Princess Elizabeth and Princess Margaret Rose. Ma sat by a lamp and opened the letter she'd received from Bob Curry that afternoon. It was dated August 4. He was responding to the letter that she'd forwarded from Dad about his interest in Stockbridge. The letter began:

Dear Anne,

Your letter of July 27 arrived yesterday, and I open each letter with trembling hand in hopes that the first line will give us the glad news that Al is out of Communist territory. . . . Bishop Bentley informed Bishop Lawrence that the National Council has just been informed from Hankow that Al would be returning to the States at his earliest opportunity. Appie Lawrence is favorable to Al's looking into Stockbridge. . . . Hoping that Al will get back here in September or early October at the latest. . . . I can well understand how you hate to leave before Al gets out, and didn't really think that you would be coming at the end of July, but we want you to know that we are ready to receive you at any moment of the day or night, in any week, in any month.

He filled her in on news of his wife Betty and New England and ended saying, *"This rapid transit of letters over so many miles is certainly wonderful and we feel that we are in close contact with you and right up with the news. We all send our love and continued prayers. Always, Bob"*

It was indeed miraculous that a letter to the States could take a little over a week while telegrams between Wuchang and Hong Kong took over four days — their delivery was uncertain even at that. His newsy letter was like a magic cord linking her to home. But Stockbridge was surely a dream that would never come true. They'd never make it by September, that she knew, even if Alfred made it out next week. She had called the President Lines. The ticket agent explained that they were jammed with refugees, but he could hold space for five on the *U.S.S. President Wilson* for a November crossing. She promised to put down a deposit the following day.

The next morning, on a thin sheet of airmail stationary, she wrote to Bob about her plan to spend a month in Lan Tao and then sail home, hopefully with Alfred, in November. She said that if Alfred was still in Wuchang, and the children were completely well when she returned from Lan Tao, she might not leave Hong Kong. She said she could not think too much about that possibility, in fact, could not contemplate it at all.

Then, before she mailed it, she picked up the thick packet of letters Dad's student had delivered and pulled one out at random to re-read it:

My Dear Wife:

I suppose that is a rather formal way to address a letter, but it is not intended to be so. The word "wife" has a very special meaning to me because of you. It reminds me of how I have for a partner in life one of the most loyal and lovable of all people on earth. It means home, and motherhood, the family circle. It carries memories of so much we have shared and how your loyalty has been my salvation. It means the one who most understands both my weaknesses and my strengths and who knows how to help the one and direct the other. It calls up memories of long walks in the evening up in Bridgeton, Maine, shared dreams and hopes, common work and mutual defense against attacks from without the fortress of our togetherness. It means moments of ecstasy – Bridgeton, Maine, the Statler – the porch here in Wuchang. It means the inexpressible comfort of simply belonging to someone and being with that person. It is a wonderful word – a term of honor – a title of love. . . . In finding you, I have found myself.

How could she possibly leave this man and wait half a world away for his return? She could not bear the idea. Yet, in all probability, that is what she would have to do for the sake of the children. She prayed that some move on her part, some decisive move – like taking a month in Lan Tao – would alter the slant of the universe, the alignment of the planets, God's will itself, and bring her husband back to safety.

In Wuchang, Dad was pacing around the kitchen in baggy khaki shorts, leather sandals flapping, a towel around his neck to catch the sweat. He was without a shirt, which rather shocked Er Lao, and he was venting his frustration at a fevered pitch, which shocked Er Lao even more. He'd never seen such an outburst!

"They tell you to come back in a week. Fine. I do that. They tell you that week to go to another place. I do that too. Nothing. Can't travel without a pass, can't get a pass to travel. I've had it up to here, Er Lao. It seemed so close last week!"

Dad stopped pacing and faced Er Lao with wild eyes. Then his face went slack. He said, "They're not going to let me out, Er Lao. What they want with me, I do not know, but they're not going to let me out, are they?" He began pacing again. "Er Lao," he said suddenly, "I want you to look into that sailboat you mentioned. I'm a good sailor. I can get down the Yangtze in a sampan or any other Chinese rig. I don't care about bombs, bandits, soldiers – any of it. I'm ready to go – whatever the risks. And I want you to stay here, out of harm's way."

Er Lao noted the panic in Dad's voice, the urgency. Dad wasn't given to broad displays like this. In fact, Er Lao had been worried about how quiet he'd grown the last few weeks – eating less and less, "down in the dumps," as Dad put it. In some ways, this frothing agitation relieved Er Lao, but he could not, would not, let him go out on his own. He'd heard too many things, too many ugly things, to imagine that anyone could make it.

The motor ferry to Lan Tao bounced and slapped up against the waves. Ma wished she'd never been born. She was sicker than she'd ever been and prayed they'd get there soon. Sally Stevens made her way along the rolling deck with word that they were almost there. The captain said there was a bad storm brewing, but they would outrun it, Sally told Ma.

"See, Ma, see? Lan Tao – we can see it!" Polly and Patty said, but Ma could not lift her head.

Finally they were on firm ground. Coolies loaded up the straw suitcases and provisions, and our party climbed into sedan chairs for the journey to the top. As the procession wound up the long paths, through the lower forests, up the mountain, the air seemed cooler with each step. At the top there was a broad reach of grassy fields, loaded with wildflowers and dotted here and there with the cinder block cottages that Sally had described, scattered about as if they had been dropped at random from a passing plane.

They made their way to the main lodge, drinking the cool air deep into their lungs. Why, it was cool enough for sweaters! Released from the confines of the swaying sedan chairs, the children bolted into the tall grasses, running and jumping like wild colts. "Lan Tao!" they shouted, "Lan Tao!"

A middle-aged Chinese man named Yin Lo led us over rolling fields, around some cliffy outcroppings to our cabin in an isolated spot farthest from the lodge. The wind was so strong, tugging at their skirts and whipping their hair, that the mothers made the children hold hands in a chain as they traversed the edge of the mountainside.

The cabin was indeed a cinder block cube, but clean and neat and hooked up with running water. At the side of the house there was a line of rope strung between two heavy poles, which filled Ma with joy at the prospect of hanging out some freshly laundered clothes. Inside, there were two bedrooms and a large front room. Some small tables and comfortable rattan chairs, padded in a cheery apricot and green fabric, filled one end of the front room. At the other end were a small kitchen and a kitchen table worn smooth. Ma checked the view from the window and asked Mrs. Stevens why there appeared to be chicken wire strung through their thick panes of glass. Sally replied brightly, "Oh, that's just for the storms – the winds can get fierce up here!" As if to punctuate the point, the front door caught the wind and slammed back against the outer wall.

Yin Lo showed them how to slip the iron rods through the heavy outer shutters to close them against the wind. He showed them how to light the stove, and where the stores of wood, kerosene for the lamps, and other supplies were kept. He reminded them that dinner was served at the lodge at 6:00, and then left by the back door. It would be the last they saw of him or anyone else for two days.

The mothers unpacked in an excited frenzy, in a charged atmosphere. The older children raced in and out, jumped on the cots, created a general nuisance, and refused to watch the little ones. Quite suddenly, in the midst of it all, the sky turned almost black, and the mothers ran out to call the children in and fasten the shutters. Rain began to pelt the house, great sweeps of it scattering across the roof and then shifting suddenly to slant sideways against the west wall.

The mothers lit the lamps, lit the stove for some tea, and reassured the children. By evening the wind no longer howled – it shrieked and raged around them. Cinder block suddenly made a lot of sense. So did chicken wire. They found some cans of food in the cupboard and took an inventory of their supplies.

Over a supper of canned soup, Mrs. Stevens raised her eyebrows at Ma and mouthed, "typhoon," rounding her lips in prolonged exaggeration on the last syllable. Ma nodded in agreement. This was no ordinary storm.

Suddenly there was a great banging by the window – one of the front shutters pulled loose from the rod. Whack! It slammed back against the outer wall, leaving half of the window exposed. The shutter careened back and forth, its hinges crying out in pain. Everyone shoved the furniture away from the window and stood back. The hinge gave way, and they watched in horror as the shutter caught the wind and flung itself straight out at an angle until the other hinge broke. The shutter hovered horizontally for a second, then crashed against the window, breaking the glass before it blew away in the wind like a piece of cardboard. Thankfully, the chicken wire kept the glass from shattering, but the rain poured in through the holes and cracks. The two women sent the children, crying and whimpering, into the back bedroom. They got all the towels they could find, and on their hands and knees, they soaked up the water. But they were themselves getting pelted and soaked in the sideways gusts, and the children were shrieking with fear. They spread the towels out and went back to the children where they huddled together, holding hands and praying they would not be blown off the mountain. They sang songs, they told stories, they prayed some more. "Father who art in Heaven, help us now, keep us safe in your hands." There in the back room they stayed, all night and all the next day and night, except for periodic forays into the front room to soak up the water on the floor or to heat up some food.

On the afternoon of the second day, they heard an alarming sound – thumping at the back door and what sounded like a muffled cry. They cautiously cracked the door open and found a man crouched on the doorstep, his face completely covered by a towel. "Come in, come in!" they cried, pulling him forward. Once inside, he slowly rose to his full height, shivering in the puddle of water rapidly forming around his feet. He removed the towel. It was Yin Lo! He told them he had crawled, mostly on his belly, the towel shielding his face from the driving rain, along the edge of the mountain to see if they were all right.

"Yes! Yes!" they said. "Yin Lo! You wonderful man!"

"Yin Lo! Yin Lo!" the children bounced around him as if he were a long-lost relative.

"Did you bring our Daddy with you, Yin Lo?" Patty wanted to know.

Yin Lo shook his head no as Ma shushed the children. "Typhoon," he said, raising his voice above the wind, stating the obvious. "I am sorry we did not know it was coming. We would not have . . ."

"That's all right. Come on now, warm yourself." Ma and Mrs. Stevens led him to the stove. He checked the window and saw it could not be fixed now.

"The typhoon will be over soon tonight, surely," he said. Then he wrapped the towel around his head once more and crawled away to check on others.

By morning, just as Yin Lo had predicted, the winds had died down to nothing and the rains had stopped. In the still-ness following the storm, the world blinked to life. Grasses began to revive, water dripped off the eaves, the sky turned a startling blue, and two little birds flew onto the roof. The damage seemed limited to the window and the clothesline, the latter of which had disappeared entirely. By late afternoon, the mothers gathered us up and set out for the main lodge.

Coming over the broad slope, they stood still and listened to the sound coming from the lodge – a hymn, a familiar hymn, "Now thank we all our God, with hearts and hands and voices!" The two mothers, exhausted and exhilarated, wept, of course. How could they not? And we children followed suit. Then we entered a dining hall full of smiling people who gladly made a space for us and kept right on singing.

Thousands of miles away in Lenox, Massachusetts, Bob Curry sat down to write to Ma with news from the Stockbridge parish. He and a committee had been fixing up the rectory, which had stood vacant for so long, with some fresh paint and repairs. He wrote, *"When we finish, it is going to be a swell house again . . . and each push I have given in the way of scrubbing and rubbing has been in the hope that the Starratts will be the next occupants."* He wrote that the junior warden of the church, who was head of the search committee, would return from vacation on September 20:

> *. . . and until that time no formal action will be taken on any other man. What we are hoping is that by this time surely Al will not only be out of Communist China, but all of you will be on your way back here if you haven't arrived. If, by the end of September, it looks as though Al will arrive in good season, the committee will wait – otherwise, in fairness to the parish, the committee will have to move in another direction. So cross your fingers and say your "Hail Marys" and get Al started.*

On September 24, four days after the junior warden came back to Stockbridge from his vacation, Dad and Er Lao, who were in Wuchang, were startled by a loud, insistent pounding on the front door. Dad was shaving and Er Lao was cooking. Philip was in his room. Er Lao opened the door, and a military officer stomped in, full of great purpose. "Find Reverend Starratt," he said as he shook a roll of papers at Er Lao.

Dad was already down the stairs, wiping his face with a towel. "Now it starts," he thought, "I'm to be hauled off to jail for some unknown offense."

To the officer he said, "I am Reverend Starratt." Er Lao stood beside him. Philip hovered in the upstairs hall, listening intently.

"You have been granted a pass to leave. These are your travel papers," the officer said. "You will leave tomorrow at 4:00 p.m. from Hankow on the *Chiang An,* a river steamer that will take you and other Americans to Shanghai. There you will board the *General Meigs,* which will take you to Hong Kong and out of China forever. You may carry one bag." He thrust the papers into Dad's hand, turned, and left without another word.

It was several minutes before Dad and Er Lao could react. Philip came racing down and took the papers from Dad's hand to look them over. Er Lao and Dad stared at each other in utter disbelief.

The shock wore off as Philip began confirming the nature of the papers. "My God," he said. "I don't believe it! You're out, Alfred. They've let you go! Wonder of wonders!"

Dad looked over the papers with Philip and then turned

to find Er Lao already upstairs, heading toward the attic for a small trunk. A day-and-a-half of farewells ensued. Dad went to see Dr. Wei, who shook his hand up and down again and again and promised him a place on staff if he ever came back. He saw as many of the others as he could. The Camps and Olive were invited for a farewell dinner, and good-byes were exchanged with any and every student he ran into on campus.

Er Lao laid out some clothes and scoured the house for precious possessions. As Dad packed books that he thought he'd need to finish his dissertation, Er Lao pulled them out, replacing them with more practical items, which my father replaced with more books. They reached a compromise and then packed a small knapsack with necessities in case he lost the small trunk. He put his dissertation in it as well.

They reviewed the list of items to be given away. Dad had already sold a few things to some of the Europeans and Chinese staying on at the Mission. He told Er Lao to take all he could and give the rest away. He left the silver with Er Lao as well, hoping he'd be able to start a small business. Er Lao refused once again to take much for himself, convinced he would be accused by friends and family of stealing, and thereby lose face altogether in the community.

On the afternoon of his departure, Er Lao accompanied him by rickshaw to the landing place for the river crossing to Hankow. The landing was crowded with river men and their sampans, rafts, and other small craft yawing about in the currents. Dad set the little trunk down and turned to Er Lao and put a hand on his shoulder. They stared at each other for some time, unable to find the words. "We will meet again, old friend, in this world or the next," Dad said finally. Er Lao bowed slightly in agreement and then stepped back as Dad turned and pulled out his travel pass to show to the armed police at the launch.

But the police refused to let him board the launch. They waved him away to bargain with the river men who began to shriek like magpies – shouting epithets, calling my father a "foreign dog," laughing and spitting at his feet, and demanding more money than my father had to make the crossing. This sport kept up for a long time, the police encouraging and enjoying it thoroughly. My father glanced at Er Lao in growing panic that he would miss the steamer in Hankow. He tried to reason with them, but it became all too clear that in the presence of the police, he would never be allowed to cross the river. He would miss his hope of escape!

An old man, a peasant in a narrow wooden rowboat, was watching the taunting and derision a few yards away, when he suddenly swung his boat around and pulled into the landing. With a quick gesture he motioned my father on board. Dad leaped forward, and Er Lao threw his case in behind him. The boat dipped a moment, and Dad hauled the trunk forward as the old man pulled on the oars.

The crowd was so astonished at this bold interference that they did nothing to stop them. The old man pulled harder. Then everyone on the landing began to shout and jump up and down. The police, in a fury, rushed over to the launch to chase them down. Mercifully, the launch was its usual, cranky self, and it was some time before it sputtered to life.

Dad and the river man were in the wide river now. Dad looked back and saw the tall figure of Er Lao walking up the slope to the road, then turning to watch their progress with his hand shielding his eyes.

Dad turned to the peasant who had rescued him. "Old man," he said, "it will be bad for you on the other side."

The man nodded and kept rowing.

"Why have you put your life on the line for a stranger, for someone you do not know?" Dad asked.

The man replied simply, "I also am a man."

Dad looked out at the churning river, at Wuchang receding behind them, and let the words settle in his heart.

At the Hankow landing, the police launch charged up to the rowboat, pushed my father aside, and led the old man away. He did not look back at my father as the police pushed and prodded him along.

There was no point trying to help, so Dad hurried along the river road, hoping against hope to make it in time. As he ran along, the air filled with the scream of an air raid siren, and soon a low-flying plane buzzed the river. Dad and the few others on the road dove for the ditch. He held his knapsack over his head in hopes that his dissertation would, at that moment, prove to be of more practical than abstract value. The bombs exploded somewhere further upriver.

He made it on time to the *Chiang An* and prayed that its name, "Forever Peaceful" or "Peace Forever," was an omen. There were about twelve Americans on board. It is not clear now if Henry Rhodes was among them. The others included a group of rather hard-boiled businessmen, a small cluster of Catholic nuns, and several members of the diplomatic corps. None of them could believe the seemingly random act of good fortune that led them to this moment, but all of them were relieved, not only for themselves, but for their Chinese friends for whom their very presence in China had begun to pose danger.

After their introductions, one of the embassy people Dad

had met a few times before said he'd heard about a Huachung theological student forced to give a speech denouncing Christianity and his foreign teachers. The student refused to read the prepared text at the last minute, the man said, and he was taken away – shot, he'd heard. "No, beheaded!" someone else said, "He was beheaded at the East Gate."

The man continued, "I was wondering – was he one of your students?"

"Yes, he was," Dad said and looked away. He would not elaborate and refused to speak further of it. He squeezed his eyes shut at the unbearable memory of that afternoon. The student, Li Shan To, was one of the boys who had come after class so long ago to ask about being baptized, and whom the bishop had baptized in May. It was not known what had become of him after he was taken away. Dad tried never to know. And now, as Hankow slipped behind a curve in the river, he'd found out.

The steamer, an easy target for the Nationalist bombers, set out with the plan of traveling by night and pulling into port during the day in places that had anti-aircraft guns. Sometimes the Americans were taken for their own safety to a local prison. Sometimes they stayed on the steamer under guard. It is not clear how many days they traveled in this fashion, but all went well at first. Then on a perfectly clear night, the ship ran aground in the middle of the river in a well-marked area. The crew and the Chinese passengers were ferried off by soldiers, but the Americans were ordered to stay on board the foundering ship. Apparently it was not in danger of sinking, but they would be hard to miss come daylight. It was clear they could not disobey the order by trying to get to shore. Many in the party began to suspect sabotage. They figured they'd been left there with what would become a convenient explanation for their demise. They would be blown to bits by the Nationalists, supported by U.S. aid and armaments, and the Communists would not have to bother with them further.

At the first light of dawn, the businessmen and diplomats approached my father and said, "Look, Reverend, you better use all your powers, all your connections. We're sitting ducks here."

"What do you want me to do?" Dad asked. He was desperately trying to keep his own fear in check.

"Pray for rain, of course!" one of the businessmen replied. The others nodded vigorously.

"It's our only hope, see? Keep the bombers from seeing us. You've got to help us," they said.

Pray for rain?? My father was astonished. He did not believe in praying for concrete things like rain, he explained. Why, it was like a child praying for a new bicycle!

Then he looked at their frightened faces and at the nuns, watching him expectantly, already forming a circle, some getting on their knees. Who was he to suspect he had a superior vision, a more informed and intelligent concept of prayer? Who was he to sweep aside the faith of others? Who was he to know God's mind?

He walked over to them and bowed his head. He prayed for rain. He prayed for cloud cover. He prayed that they would be kept safe in the boat on the river. He asked that God look on them with favor in their hour of need. They held hands as he led them in the 23rd Psalm, "The Lord is my shepherd, I shall not want. . . . " some of them faltering over the words. And the deep sense of communion among their circle humbled him.

Dawn broke to a low, gray cloud cover. Aircraft engines droned overhead, above the clouds. Dad continued to pray as the first drops of rain splattered on the upturned faces of the little circle on the foredeck. They listened to the bombers all that day as the rain continued to fall.

At the main pier in Hong Kong Harbor, Ma was checking with the harbor master. The last of the passengers had disembarked from the *General Meigs*. Her husband was not among them. Just back from Lan Tao, she had received a telegram from the Mission in Wuchang, dated September 25, telling her that Dad had set sail for Shanghai that day. The relief she felt was indescribable. The American embassy had reported that the *General Meigs* was taking Americans out of Shanghai in a last-ditch effort and that Dad might be on it. The harbor master reviewed the passenger list again, and again found Dad's name was crossed off. He hadn't made it. But the man agreed to call Ma with news of any ship en route to Hong Kong from Shanghai. He told her not to give up hope and offered other words of encouragement, but they both knew how much damage the Nationalist bombers were doing to steamships on the Yangtze.

In Stockbridge, the junior warden, the search committee, and the vestry agreed that they could not wait any longer. It was already October, and they needed to fill the position. They would start interviewing again for a new rector. Bob

Curry came home to find his wife Betty putting plants to bed for the winter in her garden. They commiserated over the inevitable and expressed deep concern over Alfred's fate.

On the Yangtze River, a group of soldiers was taking the Americans, still alive and well, off the *Chiang An* and loading them into smaller craft for a night sail to a small port down-river. There they were marched to the town prison and held, for their own safety, it was said. They were given a meal and assurances that they would be put on the next train for Nanking. The following day, as the departure time drew near, no one came for them, and they feared they had been left there through some failure of communication, or perhaps by design. Their cells had been left unlocked, though, so they devised a plan. One of them knew the way to the station, and they decided that if they walked in formation as a group, they would so boldly attract attention that it would appear that they were either prisoners or had been given some official clearance. The jailer looked the other way as they marched off to the station, two by two. Amazingly, the plan worked, and they arrived without incident just as the train was beginning to pull out. They threw their belongings into a passing boxcar. Several men hoisted themselves in and pulled up the women, with help from those on the ground who were momentarily enveloped by the nuns' long black robes. Then they ran along beside the car and hopped aboard themselves. They rolled away from the open doors just as a jeep loaded with police, blowing their whistles and waving their guns, pulled up to the train. But the engineer ignored the whistles and kept moving.

A long journey in the boxcar took them finally to Nanking. Dad got off and showed the local police his pass. As the officials on one side of the train busied themselves reviewing his papers and making up their minds if he was legal and could pass on, the rest of his party unloaded the bags on the opposite side of the train and moved quietly to a coach car and passed their baggage up to the willing arms of the passengers on board. As the whistle sounded "all aboard," the police were diverted by some commotion in the station. They left Dad to climb on board. He grabbed a seat near his friends, and soon the Chinese passengers in the car, observing both their activity and their condition, shared food and water with the group.

By the time they reached Shanghai, the *General Meigs,* the American repatriation ship, had already sailed. They then learned that a French ship, the *Maréchal Joffre,* was sailing the following day. The French didn't want to take them on board, afraid of reprisals for smuggling Americans to Hong Kong, but the French might look the other way if they sneaked on as stowaways. They took the risk, and the group got into the hold of the ship around midnight. The engines started up in the morning, and with that great shuddering sound, they knew they were at last sailing to freedom. There was nothing to eat, but they found some water, which they gave to the nuns. The rest of them opened bottles of *vin ordinaire.* As they drank it, the diplomats sang an old favorite of the diplomatic corps, "Oh it's wine, wine, wine that makes you feel so fine in the corps, in the corps!" Soon, even the nuns were joining in the chorus.

They arrived in Hong Kong late at night. Everyone pressed against the railing, looking at the glowing city, at the line of lights strung up like beads to the top of Victoria Peak. Hong Kong – shimmering, nearly incandescent. There simply were no words for it. Eventually, a Chinese man leaning on the railing next to my father said quietly, "Huan ch'en ti-quo chu-ee!" (Long live foreign imperialism!)

Dr. Harth handed the phone to Ma. It was the harbor master again. A French ship, the *Marèchal Joffre,* was coming into the harbor that night, and passengers would be ferried off around 10:00 the next morning, he said. Reverend Starratt was not on the advance passenger list, but one never knew. "We'll be there," Ma said.

She was waiting with the three of us at the landing dock when the launches began bringing off the passengers. She tried to see if she could make out a familiar head, a familiar shape, among the crowd on the first launch. Then she caught her breath, held her hand to her mouth.

She could never tell the whole story of that reunion. She could get to the part about how my father climbed out of the launch, a bit unsteady, a bit thin, a knapsack on his back, how he started up the long wharf. She could tell how she let Polly and Patty run ahead of her, how my father bent down and engulfed them in his open arms, how she stood, unable to move, as I toddled toward him. How we children clambered over him as he knelt there, how he looked up at her with tears streaming. But there her story would end. It was understood that no words could capture the wonder of that moment between them. It was understood that in that moment we were all blessed beyond measure.

$\mathcal{S}even$

ONE CAN IMAGINE the mixed feelings my parents had a month later as they stood on the deck and watched Victoria Peak fade into the mist as the *U.S.S. President Wilson* steamed out of Hong Kong Harbor. Beneath us in the hold were the three or four trunks with the few belongings we still owned. Before us lay the vast Pacific Ocean and an uncertain future.

As she said she would, my mother kissed the ground when we arrived in San Francisco several weeks later. We took the California Zephyr to Chicago, and then another train to Boston, where Bob Curry picked us up. He beamed and beamed and caught us up in his broad arms, gave us all a bear hug, and laughed in his great and wonderful way. In the car as he took us to Lenox, he told Dad that they'd continued the search in Stockbridge, but hadn't found anyone that met their satisfaction. They were still looking. "So if you're still interested . . . " he said, and all the adults laughed.

My father preached the following Sunday at St. Paul's in Stockbridge, Massachusetts. He stood in the pulpit for some moments before he could gain his composure. He thought of Er Lao, of all their friends so far away, who now filled his heart in the prayer, "Bless all those we love who are absent from us." Softly, almost inaudibly, he began with a prayer. The congregation leaned in and his words grew stronger. He told them of his journey, his long journey to this place, of the simple acts of courage he'd witnessed, acts of kindness that crossed religious boundaries and political barriers. He talked about losing heart and finding it again in faith.

At the end of the service, he stood outside on the stone entryway with Bob, and one by one the congregation shook his hand, shook the hand of this man they had heard so much about for so long. They welcomed this young missionary and his family as if they were greeting one of their own. The vestry was so favorably impressed that they dispensed with the usual deliberation and offered him the job that afternoon. My father was so impressed with the people of St. Paul's that he accepted on the spot, forgetting to ask what the salary might be.

After visiting relatives in Boston for about two weeks, my parents had our three or four small trunks shipped to Stockbridge, packed our straw suitcases, and set out for the rectory where we faced the prospect of starting over. There was no moving van behind us and none to come. We had no furniture, no linens, not so much as a pot or pan.

And so it was that we pulled into the driveway on that

snowy evening of December 22. Perhaps we sat there a moment to catch our breath, stunned into silence at the sight of the light flooding from every window of the white clapboard house. We took it as a sign of a friendly welcome from the Church so we would not have to enter the empty house in the dark.

I can imagine my mother collecting herself, adjusting her hat, and bustling up to the front door, we children racing ahead, my father following in slow steps. I can imagine the catch of a sigh in her throat of both relief and anxiety as we prepared to enter the well-lighted, but bare, rooms of a house that had stood vacant for months. The confluence of emotions must have been dramatic as she opened the door.

Nothing could have prepared us for what we found. There in the living room was a twinkling of tinsel and ornaments glittering softly from the branches of a six-foot-tall Christmas tree. Near the fireplace were chairs, a sofa, and end tables. There was a rug on the floor. My sisters raced upstairs to find fully-made beds in each room and bureaus and lamps and real feather pillows. Shrieks from the girls brought my father up after them, where he found them hugging dolls that had been left for them on their beds – not old, used dolls out of a missionary barrel, but brand new ones with curly hair and eyes that blinked.

What brought us downstairs again was a wonderful smell from the kitchen that filled the house. There we found my mother weeping into a cloth kitchen towel with her back to the stove. She could not speak. She could not look at us. She merely pointed behind her to the stovetop where there was nothing less than a loaf of fresh bread and a gently bubbling stew.

We gathered, we five, my sisters clutching their dolls, into a family hug. My mother was the first to break away, blowing her nose and busying herself with distributing the stew onto the plates already laid out on the kitchen table. It was then that my father took my hand, and with Polly and Patty, we went into the living room to look at the tree. Perhaps I hung back a bit, envying the girls their new dolls and overwhelmed by the emotion flooding around us all. I don't know. But what I do remember was that the lights from the tree revealed a single object underneath the heavy bottom branches – a cloth doll with a blue dress and a plaid bow in her yarn hair with a note "for Penny." Whoever had put it there must have assumed I would not be able to reach up to my bed to find her.

My mother called us with a joyful, "Supper's ready!" and we sat down at the kitchen table and bowed our heads. My father said grace, my mother adding to it as she always did, but this time there was almost too much to be thankful for.

The people of Stockbridge had gathered their forces, and in less than two weeks, had furnished our house from top to bottom. Not just the parishioners of St. Paul's, but the *whole* town. The old hotels, Heaton Hall and the Red Lion Inn, contributed linens and beds. The local garage gave tools. Brahmin's variety store gave bolts of material, and women sewed them into curtains. Summer residents were contacted at their winter homes and contributed various pieces of furniture and the dolls. And from all over town people brought cookware and plates, sofas and chairs, tables and lamps, rugs and bookshelves from their own homes. No money was exchanged and no profit was made, except the profit that returns from a gift of love.

The furnishings were ours to keep, and some remain in our family today. Far more important, of course, was the lasting imprint of life's essential goodness. When the world seems a weary place, when I struggle, as we all do, to make sense of its darker side, a light filters through the shadows. It is more than a memory. It is an internal space that softens cynicism and nurtures hope. Our Stockbridge homecoming, our welcome from people we did not know and had not met, was as life-altering and as eloquent as the deceptively simple words, "I also am a man," spoken by an old Chinese peasant to a stranger crossing the Yangtze River in a narrow wooden rowboat.